High Shelf

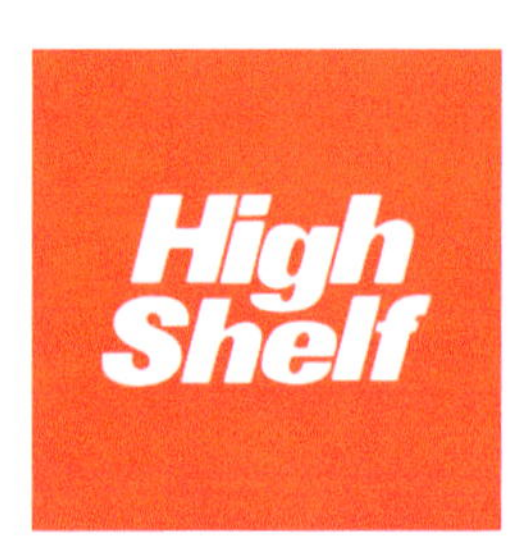

High Shelf Issue VIII 2.8.19

Portland, Oregon.
Copyright 2019, High Shelf Press

ISBN: 978-1-7330279-5-3

Cover Image by Linda Briskin
Design and Layout by C. M. Tollefson
Edited by Angela Dribben & C. M. Tollefson

High Shelf VIII

July 2019

"...my instincts are
calamitous &i

frequently
overstep

the boundaries
of strangers..."
Zoe Canner

Table Of Contents

Lachesis

Annie Woods

Find me. Find me like the definition of the biggest word you could think of in the glossary of an outdated middle school science book. I am becoming my mother because that is what puberty does. I'm growing into her ovaries like hand-me-down shoes. I think she's a fucking psycho but she's just a funhouse mirror at the end of a long day. I'm contorting to reimagine pain as genius. But all hurt is just hurt. Flip me open. Find me here, there, and everywhere.

The Scene When You Learn Nothing's About You

Melinda Winograd

Arrival and departure are simulacra of a dimension you can only smell,
        its paramnesia the ghost under your nose
        skimming the cilia of your inorganic incarnation.

Were you and I ever not the same
      event horizon
           a gravity feeding from the wreckage of our wake
              or are we waked
        here
            we they   she   me

Were you and I ever not
      just simulations of solemnity
            fernweh
         a physic law
           ache caving intimate   slam

Departure and arrival are the facsimile of a savory desire,
      an archetypal ornamentation of unknown things
      never passing, never moving. Platitudes for the living.

ABOUT THE WEATHER

Linda Eve Diamond

Somehow seeing eye to eye
turned into choosing sides.

At least we can still talk
about the weather.

There's a nice breeze today, I say.
She says, *Ugh. There's no breeze.*

I say we can agree to disagree.
She says I'm wrong.

Seems we can't even
talk about the weather.

Stomachs rumble as storms brew.
Hearts thunder, pound and crack.

Lightning flashes in half-closed eyes.
Floods stream down heat-flushed cheeks.

A front moves in so cold we're adrift
in icy waters.

The fog between us is so thick
we disappear.

Onrush

Charise Hoge

In the recovery of words
some are birds,

a covey of adjectives:
full-throated, backlit, furtive,

without the testimony of verbs.

Sneaker Waves

Robert Grant

Here at this beach that slowly slants
away from the security of rock and tree—

then, under cover of water, gives out
suddenly like an anchor—the ocean can seem

harmless, even soothing, predictably caressing
the shore, lulling with its leisurely lapping.

Do not be fooled say the locals *Do not be fooled.*
Even violent men can appear tender for a time.

Wave Paintings
Gwen Pryor

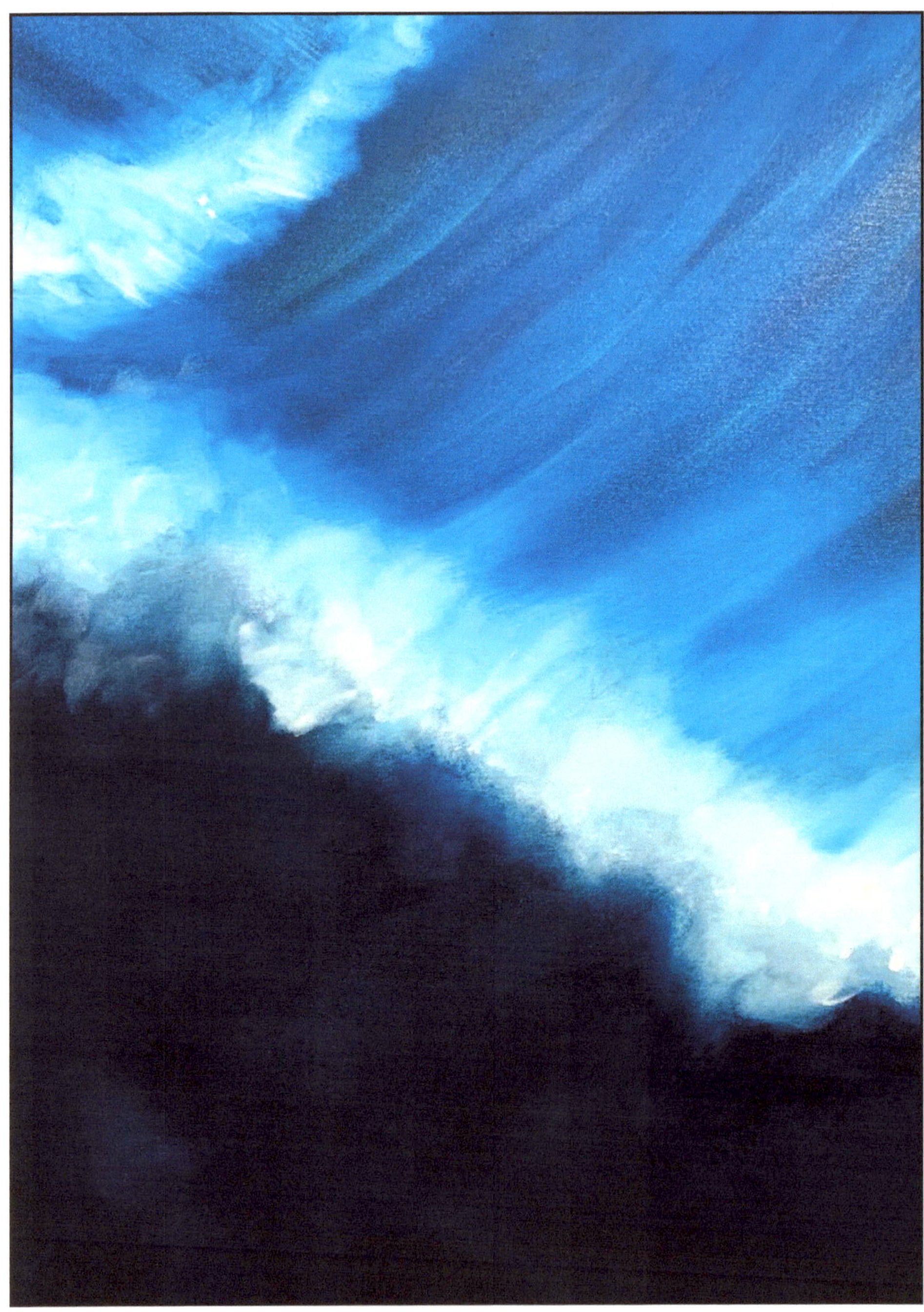

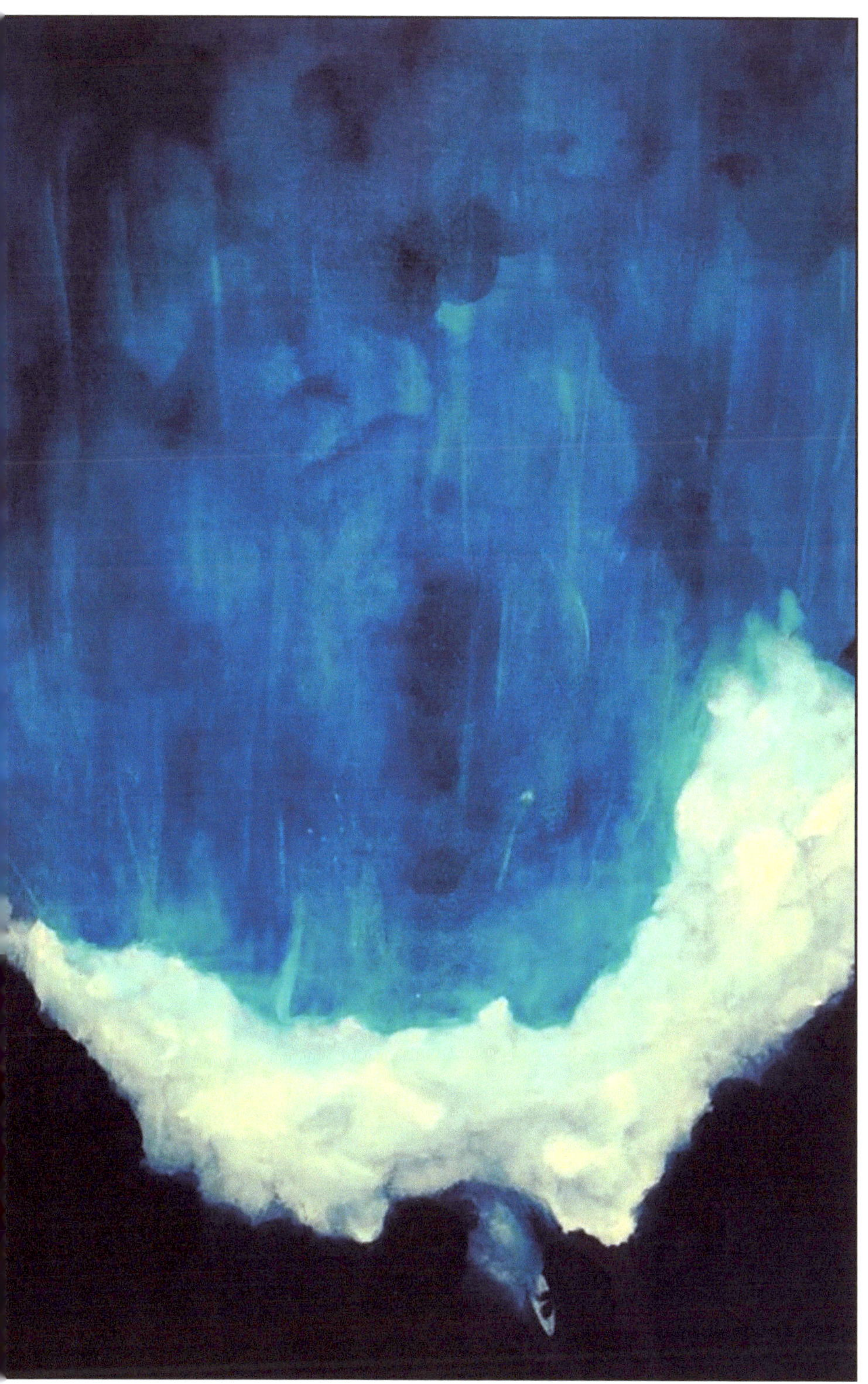

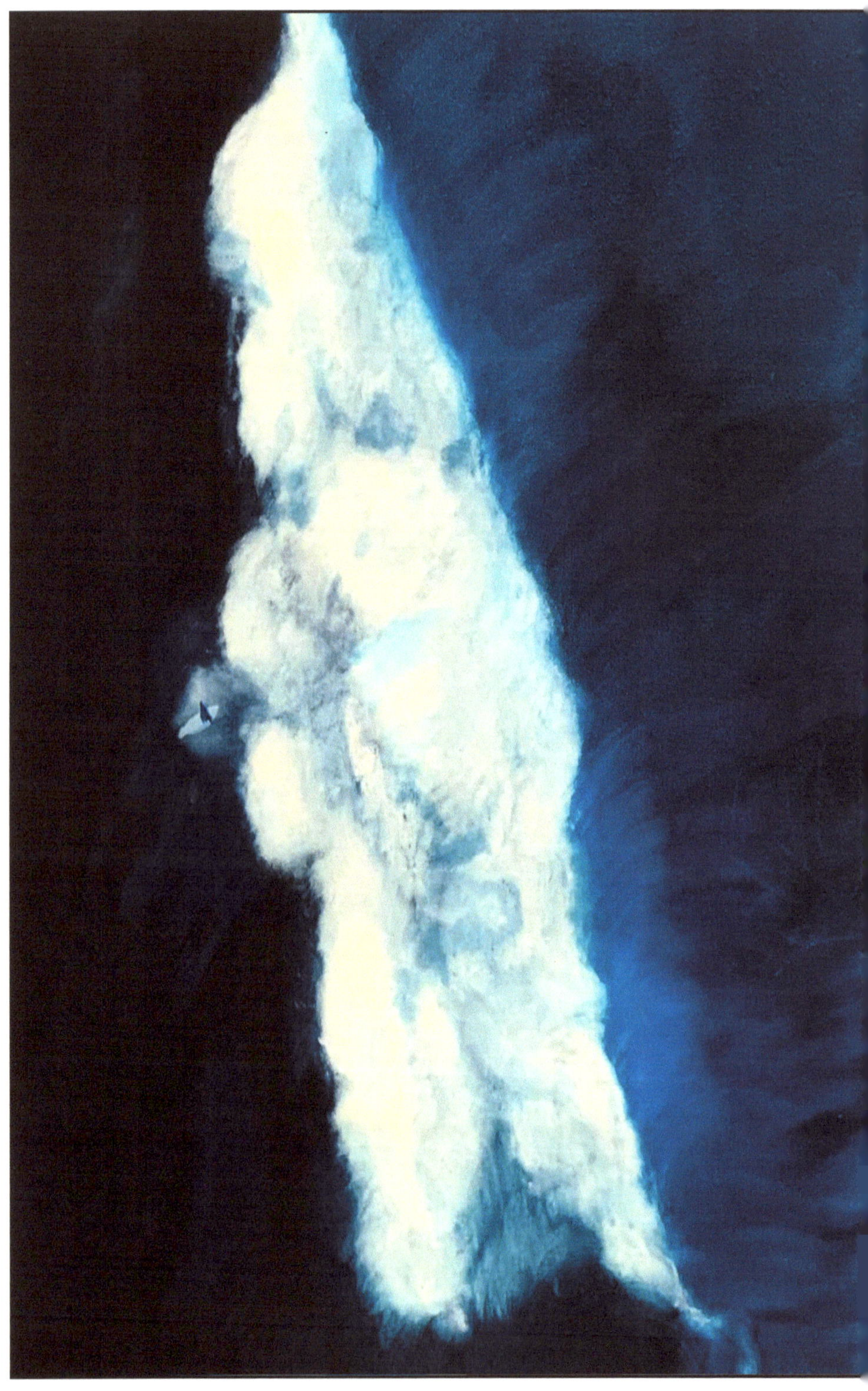

The End
Nick Lopez

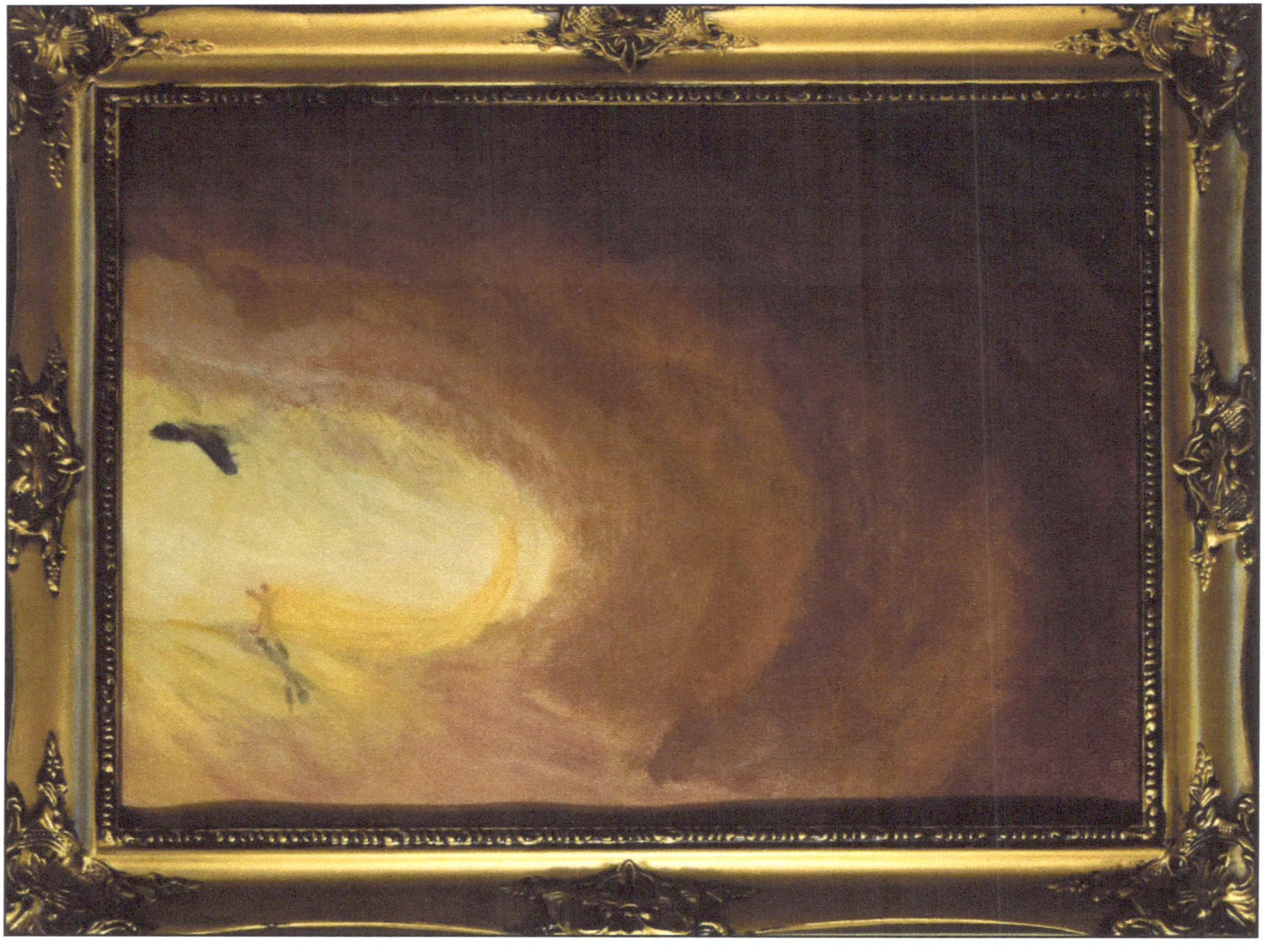

Poemolator, The

Ian Wilson

No Americans suffer more from their inability to understand, or make themselves understood by, non-English speakers than America's poets in Iraq. That's why this year The Poetry Foundation of America (TPFoA) equipped hundreds of them with the Poemolator, a hand-held electronic device that allows the poets to deliver dozens of poems, prerecorded in Arabic, to the Iraqis they encounter.

The gadget, which looks like an larger than usual television remote control -- with a speaker and a microphone on top -- bursts into Arabic when it hears an equivalent phrase in English spoken by a poet whose voice it recognizes. But like an electronic parrot, the Poemolator simply repeats what it's been programmed to repeat. Sample poem excerpts include:

> That after many wanderings, many years
> Of absence, these steep woods and lofty cliffs,
> And this green pastoral landscape, were to me
> More dear, both for themselves and for thy sake!

Fine sentiments perhaps, but of questionable value considering the state of things in the country-side. Or this:

> Despite of wrinkles this thy golden time.
> But if thou live, remember'd not to be,
> Die single, and thine image dies with thee.

Equally fine and equally troubled. And the more contemporary:

> I can't remember my name nor can you.
> Now whispers.
> Call me Wee Willie, Sir I, the senator of nonsense,
> the congressman of incoherence, dadadadada -- just so
> we're all on the same lacuna.

As a "Language Poem," this one has its own problems. Still the device's supporters claim that because the poems are prerecorded by native speakers and not computer-generated, the readings have "a more natural feel." The Poemolator is marketed as a "complete solution for cross-cultural consciousness."

Its creators at the TPFoA-financed company PoemTek do admit that even the new model, the X2, has a drawback: it is still just a "one-way" translation device. That means it renders English perfectly well into Arabic (or any of the 61 other "goal languages" it has mastered so far), but the device is no better at understanding foreign languages than the American poets who are wielding it. So the Poemolator may allow poets to read their work, but it does not help them understand any of what the listeners may have to say in response. In the case of the so-called "Language Poetry" above, that may be a real problem when the goal is not making sense.

A consumer model is expected soon.

Dear Stars

Katie Fesuk

From his second grade teacher,
my nephew learns about hieroglyphs,
scrawls from another country and era.
He likes the ones with wings.
"A is a bird," he says.
"Lots of hieroglyphs are birds."
Neither time nor place
can change our desire
to see words take flight,
feathered utterances
in a blue expanse of sky,
language turned to ibis and gull.
When he speaks of canabic jars,
I imagine women writing with kohl
on their own faces.
"C is a cup tilted sideways
with tea pouring out."
Yes, the pouring in, holding heat,
letting go.
He draws a tomb and pyramids,
remembers more: M is an owl.
Cryptic, stormy predator
my mother keeps writing
from spirit world to my own,
hooting in its tree off Hadaway Road.
M for Mary, cosmic love letter
from my daughter's namesake
flying past the Japanese maple
we planted after she died.
Dear stars, forgive me how much
I comb my child's long hair,
the color of each good sunset,
its silk in my grip,
her every sound a dove
cupped in hand,
carved into the mountains around us,
bird heartbeat in my palms.
Feathers everywhere I go.

Eligibility Questionnaire for the Temporary Aid to Climate-Impacted Deserving Poor Benefits Program

Ashley Shelby

Eligible Impacted Individuals who have been granted Designated Pauper status may receive up to three months of federally funded carbon credits, food vouchers, and housing assistance under the Temporary Aid to the Climate-Impacted Deserving Poor Program. All applicants must have a Climate Refugee Resettlement Number (CRRN) and be registered with the United States Department of Environmental Migrant Management. *This form must be filled out in the presence of a Citizen Anti-Fraud Monitor and notarized.* All answers are Yes/No and must be answered truthfully under penalty of perjury.

1) Are you a citizen of the United States?
If No, do not continue

2) Have you been convicted of a misdemeanor or a felony?
If Yes, do not continue

3) Have you ever received or sold stolen Personal Carbon Allotment (PCA) cards?
If Yes, do not continue

4) Did you complete the federally required education module "Protect Your Children By Not Having Them"?
If you have internet access and answered No, do not continue; if you do not have internet access and answered No, see the Citizen Monitor for further instruction before continuing.

5) Are you or have you ever been one of the following subgroup of Late-Stage Denier: Rapture Denier (you believed climate change was real but that it was "God-caused"); Bought Denier (you received compensation for arguing for "natural vari ation"); Legacy Denier (you were psychologically damaged by the cognitive dis sonance resulting from decades of far-right media indoctrination followed by the catastrophic effects of First Impact and can provide documentation from a licensed therapist)?
If Yes to Rapture Denier or Bought Denier, do not continue. If Yes to Legacy Denier, see Citizen Monitor for additional paperwork before continuing.

6) Do you have a food-bearing garden: windowsill garden, rooftop garden, backyard garden, a plot in a community garden?
If Yes, continue. If No, continue (this is a demographic question that has no bearing on your eligibility)

7) Do you agree with the following statement: "The welfare of each Impacted Indi vidual would best be promoted by having him solve his own problem through nor mal banking and commercial channels?"
If Yes, continue. If No, see the Citizen Monitor for reeducation materials before continuing.

When you have completed this form, please bring it to the Citizen Anti-Fraud Monitor, who will notarize it and provide you with the application form (if eligible). Please note that benefits are not guaranteed and are granted at the discretion of the Department of Environmental Migrant Management. Citizenship status, criminal background, and the applicant's Personal Documented Climate Change Rhetoric Score will be assessed by the Domestic Refugee Solutions Committee in conjunction with your application.

i saw the scar across the realtor's wrist

Zoe Canner

i saw the long
recent scar

across the
realtor's wrist

and i wanted
to kiss it

but didn't

my instincts are
calamitous &i

frequently
overstep

the boundaries
of strangers

i saw her sweet
eye contact &i

ran my fingers
over the new

pearl-shaped
bump on the

landscape
of my own

unending
forehead

instead

February 23, 2018

Tiffany Promise

Jonathon,

You should be thirty-three today, Jesus' age,
Gran-Gran's dreaded *thirty-through*.
Instead, you're eight months passed
and I know each moment like I know my baby's soft spot.
As her skull hardens, yours becomes dust.

I was thirty-eight weeks pregnant—a whole universe inside—
while you were breathing only by machine.
The others encircled (plugs/tubes/tears)
but I couldn't risk labor on a plane.

You'd weathered the chops—so ripe with trauma
it's a wonder your skin didn't slip right off (mine did)—
only to be outdone by the silly kitchen floor:
skull-buster, brain-bleeder, ender of a fucking era.

Posey stitched on your blood pressure cuff,
you two were together in the deep in-between:
playing Pogs, cold-cut-snacking, hijinks for days,
before the old switcharoo: earth to moon, Moon to earth.

In June, we'll celebrate Poe's first year,
her face smashed in trés leches, balloons to fill the room.
As she eats avocado, learns to walk, says *ghost, cracker, angel*
I'll remember that pepper-sniffing, *yoke*-tongued boy you were,
blondie bear, stinky pot, little brother.

With her every inch, your void gulfs.

Thens
Tara Cronin

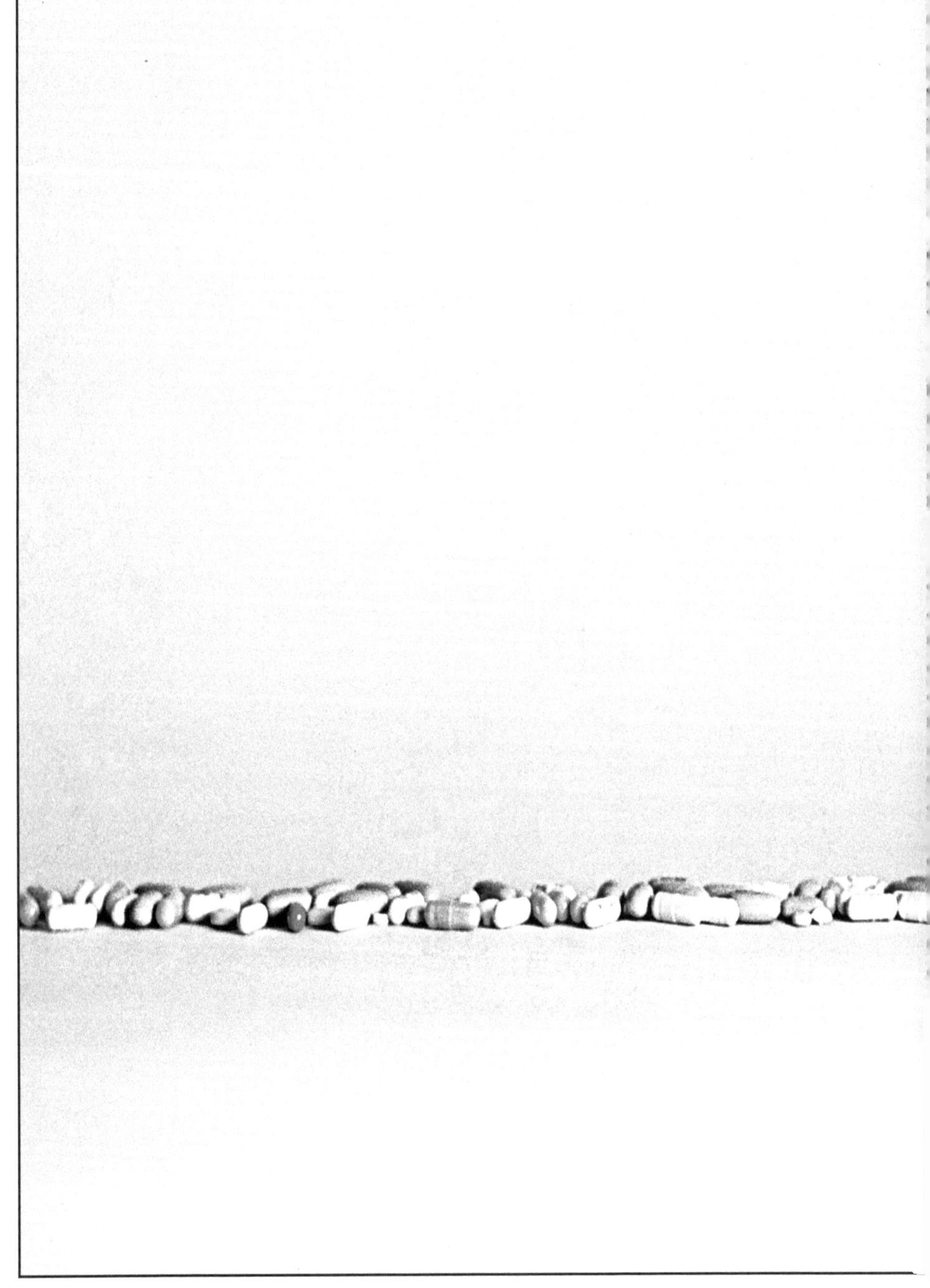

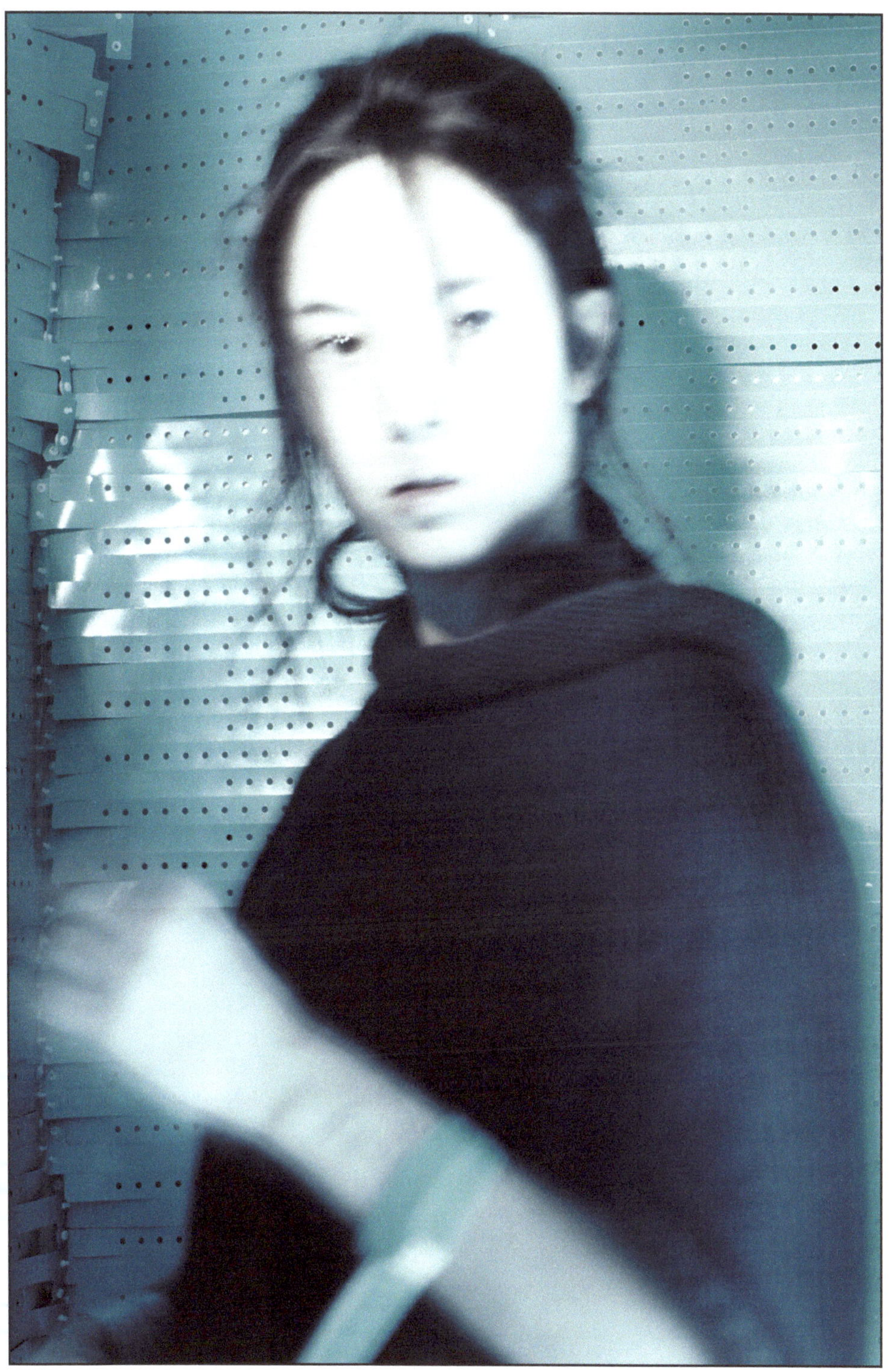

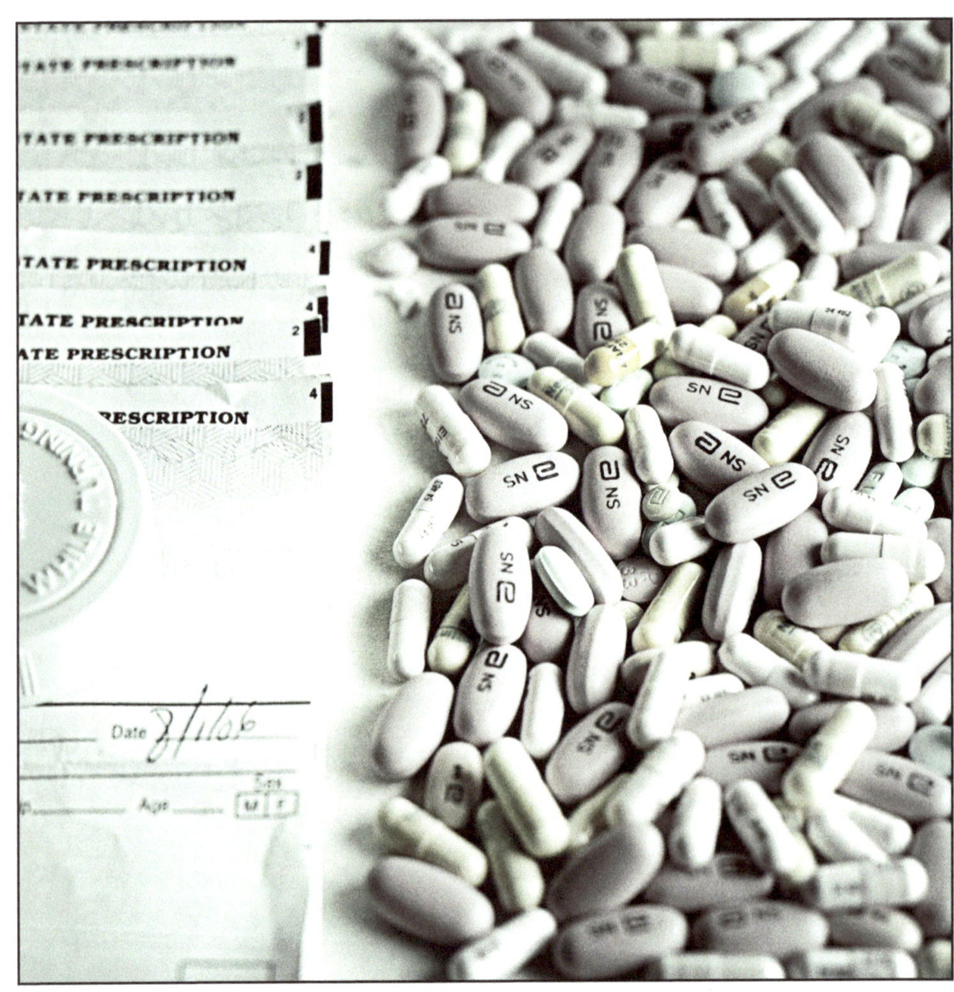
TATE PRESCRIPTION
TATE PRESCRIPTION
TATE PRESCRIPTION
TATE PRESCRIPTION
TATE PRESCRIPTION
ATE PRESCRIPTION
PRESCRIPTION
Date
Age
Sex
M F

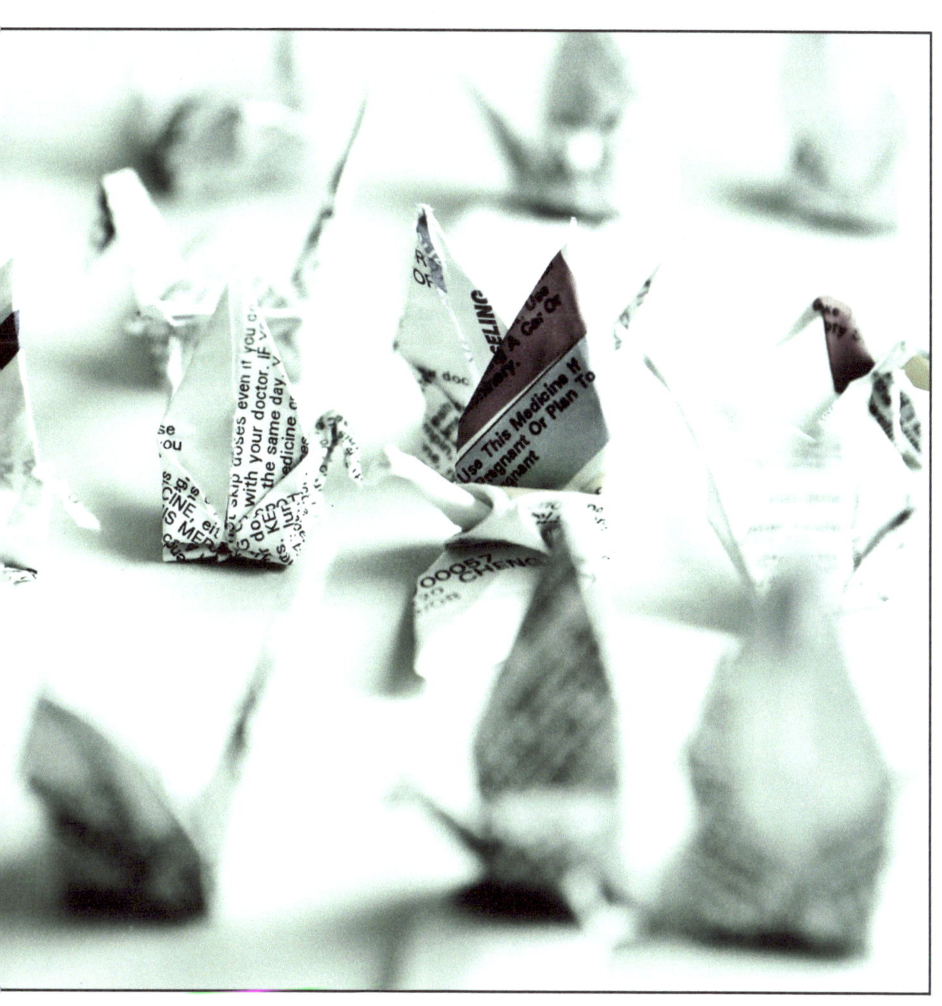

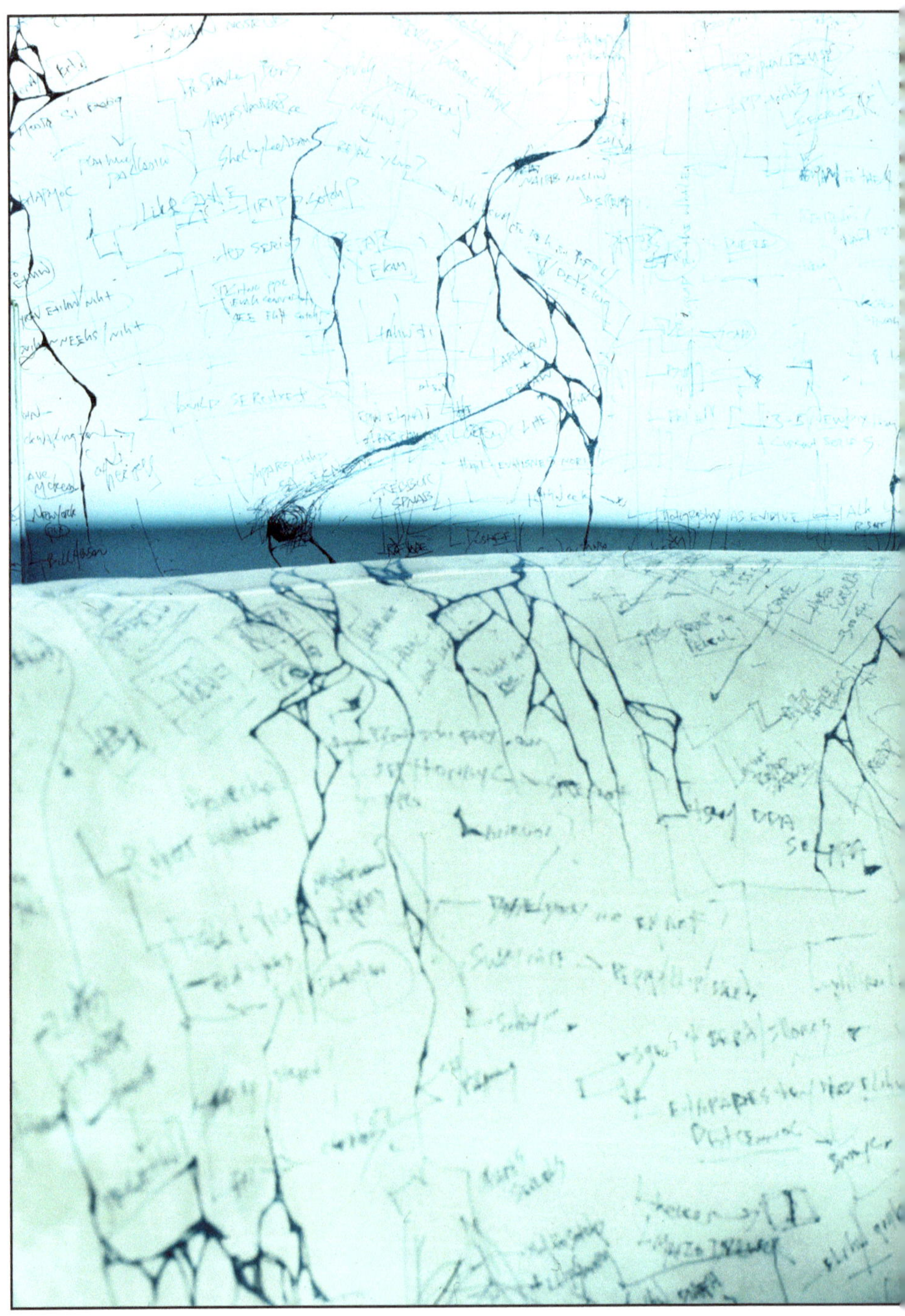

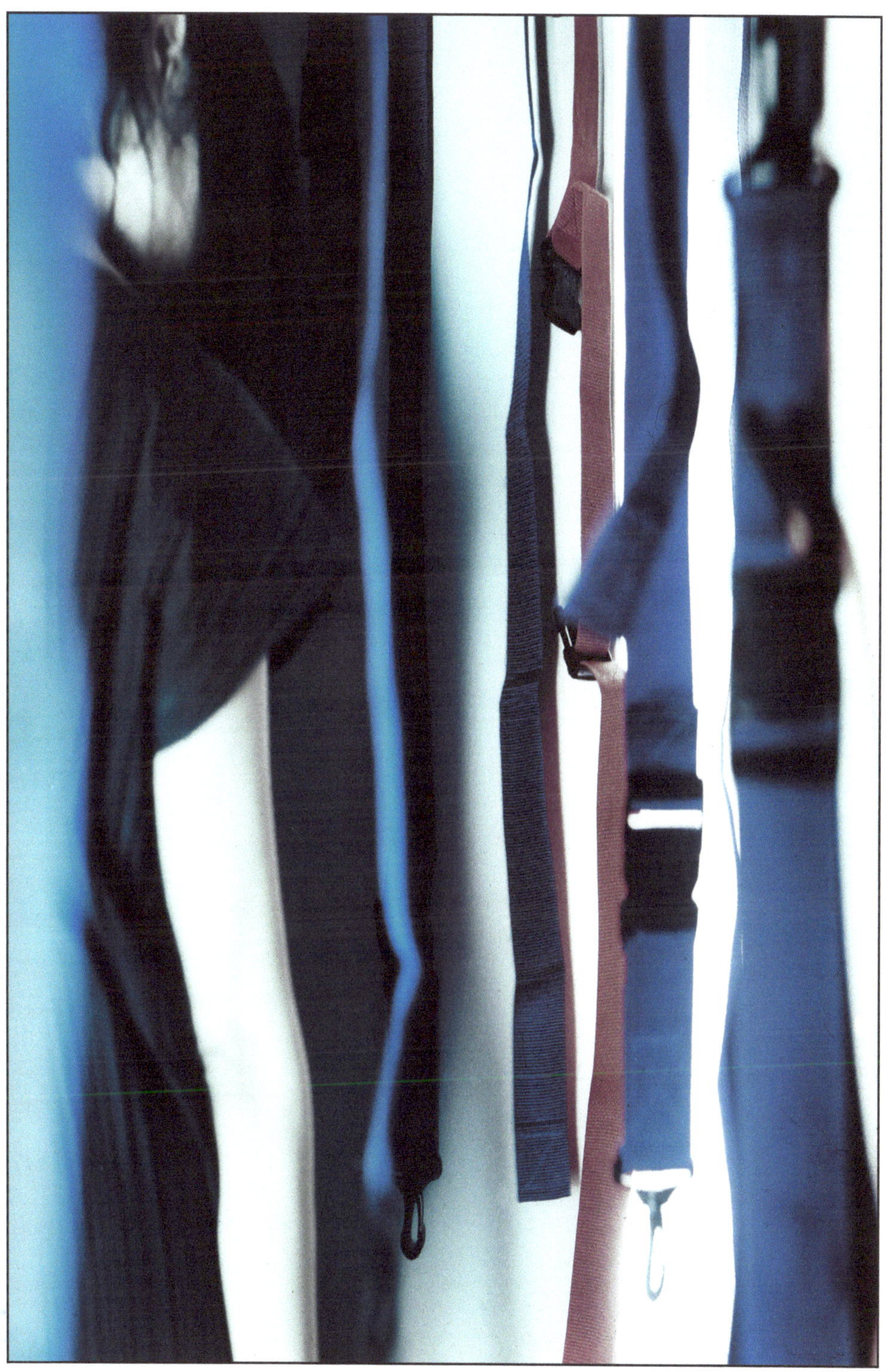

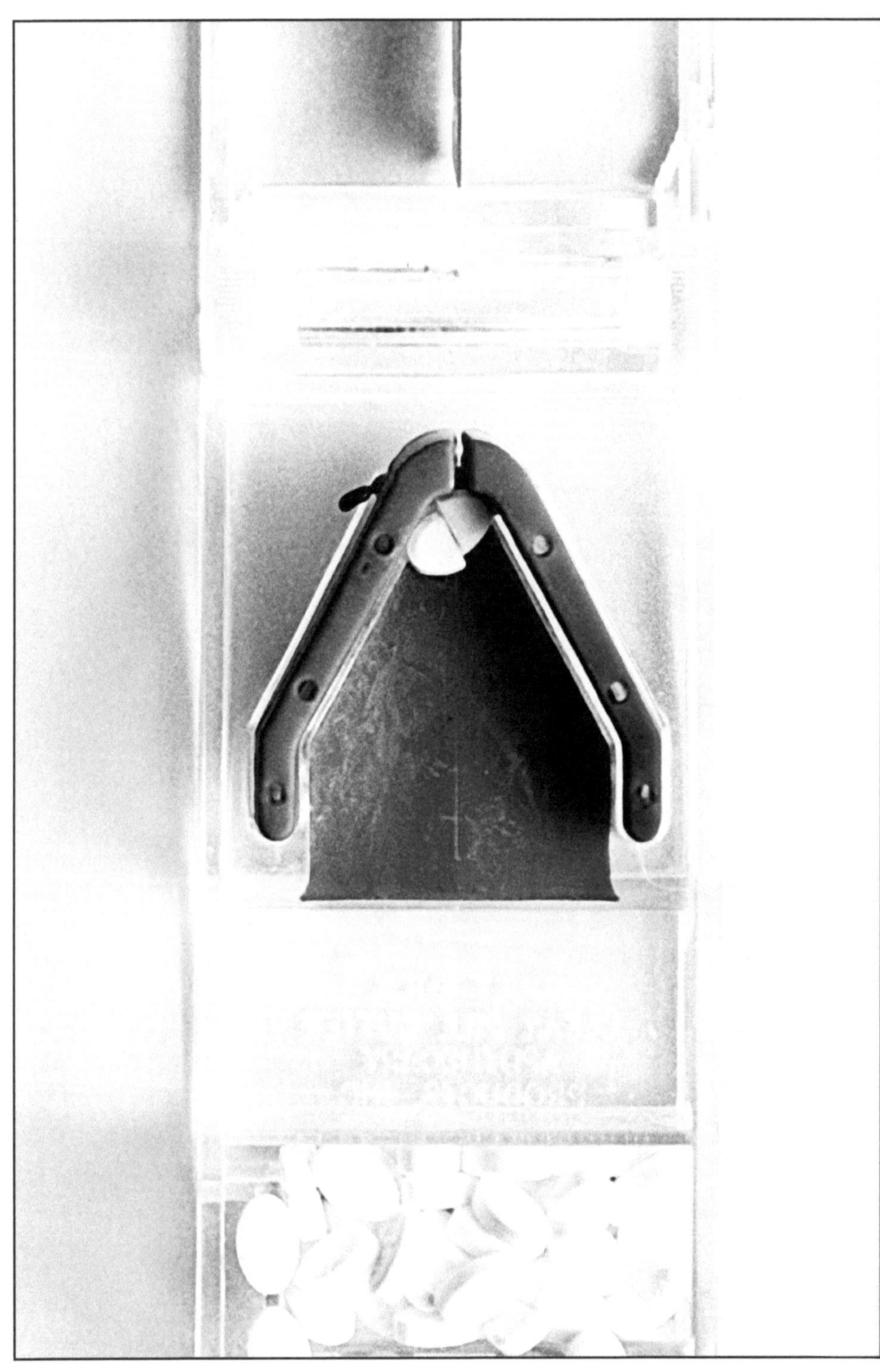

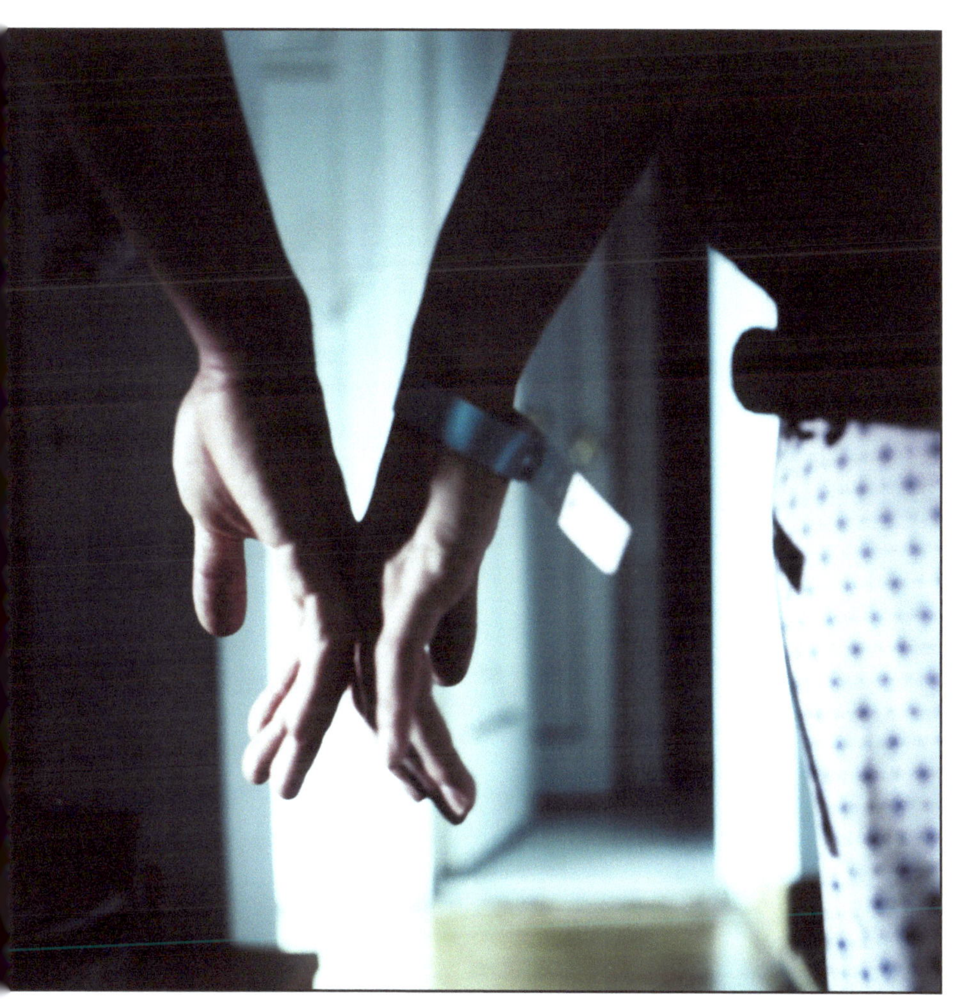

But...wait!

Nicole Schoonbrood

seriously ask yourself
delivering thanks to their Majesty:

do plants blow kisses to bees?

sneaking through heads of trees:
soaking up the Light of day:

where do Clouds plan to hijack Sun's spotlight?
what does she do when Moon sticks around?
has she even met the Stars? those pretty faces
how absorbed they are ~ *oh*
I am *sure* she would shed a tear

seriously ask yourself
as if to mock those sticks in the mud
next to Fern bathing in Mother's rays
as if he heard them gossiping
flowers reaching above his head:

how does it make Soil feel?

seriously ask yourself
in their cocoon of expired
beliefs and exhausted dreams:

what do doubts sound like?

our Eyes crave fumes of feasts: soaking up
handfuls of potatoes and garlic could never
suffice for tongues hanging by the greed of lips:

could they ever forget the taste of regret?

Risks reek of sour milk
and park beneath necks of teeth ~ *so*

what if you choke?
would you take another bite?

in my dark
Kristin Snow

in my dark
my dark
man
asks me to
put my
hands out
wait for
night rain

when it
falls says
his heart
falls with
it soft heart
of this
dark hard
man in my
wet trembling
hands

how I love
the steady
raining
man how I
love how his
heart is
now in my
hands falling no
more though
I am

The Perfect Husband

Marina Hatsopoulos

My husband Walter is in the kitchen swinging a golf club when I finally dare to bring it up again.

"It'll be fun," I say. "How often does a friend throw a birthday party in Morocco?"

"Ideally, never." He repeats his follow-through, just missing our ceiling beams. "I've already been all over the world." When put into a social setting, he'll engage—mostly by debating politics—but he'd rather be out on the course. At his age, a generation older than me, he knows what he likes. He's unmovable.

"All the husbands will be there," I insist.

"You really want me to go?" His eyes look pained.

"I don't have any *other* husbands to invite," I say, which triggers a thought: what if I did? I wouldn't want a lot of extra husbands—just three or four, so it wouldn't get confusing.

One of my husbands would love people. He'd be friends with everyone—journalists, philosophers, the Celtics, the pilot on every flight, the person who hands out towels in fancy restaurant bathrooms, plus a few U.S. presidents—and he'd get invited to all the best parties.

While he'd be out late, my introvert husband would be home writing love sonnets. Unlike Walter, who's dyslexic, this one would never ask how to spell "yoga." He'd use long words known only by the dictionary—like leptorhine, horripilation, and funambulism—and the yearning in his poetry would linger in my mind for days.

As Walter evades the Morocco decision by repeating his backswing, over and over, I put on Amy Winehouse, to which he remains indifferent. I'd have another husband who would play electric bass—raw and edgy R&B, from the heart. On stage, too cool to seek affirmation from the audience, he'd make subtle, sensual moves while looking down at his plucking fingers, oblivious to the roomful of adoration.

My final husband—because who needs more than four extras—would be a mover-and-shaker. Having built a high-speed railway across the U.S. as an entrepreneur, he'd now be working on fixing the inner-city public-school system. He'd wear fitted Italian suits, even around the house on weekend mornings. Master of the grand gesture, he'd sweep me on his private plane for an intimate catered dinner with the Dalai Lama at the Taj Mahal (India, not Vegas).

I'm delighted by all my new options for Morocco. The natural choice would be Party Guy, adored by all. Of course, he'd probably invite all the other Morocco guests—as well as our tour guide, the hotel concierge and their cleaning staff—to visit our summer home for the entire summer. Prince of small talk, he'd agree with everyone about everything. Then it strikes me that for someone who dares offer no original or controversial thought, he talks too much about too little, and the Morocco flight takes over six hours.

Back home in Boston, down in the unheated basement, Shakespeare would be writing under the light of a bare bulb. He'd wrap his cold fingers around my own, exposing his soul, his self-doubt and his anxiety, draining my body of all vitality. He wouldn't want me to leave him home alone, but even if

I could coax him past his fear of flying, how could I possibly get him through three days of humorous jabbing in Morocco by my sassy friend group?

At midnight, Bass Man wouldn't answer his phone because he'd be in a tattoo parlor having a flame etched onto his flesh. He'd offer to come to Morocco because he'd have no gigs that weekend, but hadn't he promised to find more work? For someone with such disdain for commerce, he'd sure have an appreciation of the good life (on my card). In Morocco he'd sleep during the sightseeing tours, spill room-service tagine all over the colorful tile floor, and forget his passport at a music club in Marrakech, so I'd spend the entire time cleaning up after him and bailing him out of lock-up for trying the local hashish.

I could bring Mr. Mover/Shaker, but he'd resent the conversation shifting from his recent achievement award to the Mausoleum of Mohammed V. Our friends would tease him for inviting the Stones to play at the Hassan II Mosque, but he wouldn't see the humor. Ego bruised, he'd stay up late wiring a few million dollars to a prestigious university which would already have several billion dollars, but now they could also have a building with his name on it and a new member on their board of trustees.

Then there's Walter—my real husband, in oversized sweatpants, hoping I might've forgotten about the trip in the two minutes I've been lost in my mind with my mythical husbands.

"If you want me to go, I'll go," he says.

I'd love his irreverent perspective on the sights, although the long flight would hurt his back. He doesn't do small talk, yet our crowd will be too lively for meaningful political debate. I don't want to force him on a trip that he won't enjoy; I just wish he'd want to come. Or do I? I admire his devotion to his passions. He used to drive hours every few days to snowboard, despite hips in so much pain that he hobbled to the chairlift in crutches. Indifferent to public opinion, he thinks for himself.

While he doesn't like travel, he never complains about my going without him. I can't criticize his independence, which is the very essence of my attraction to him. I can't have what I want—a partner made of rock who needs his autonomy and supports mine—and simultaneously have a husband who will want to follow me around the world.

"I'll miss you," I say, and he gives me a drawn-out, tasty kiss.

When I return, he may even surprise me with a scrawled love note thanking me for letting him off the hook (which he spells "hock").

Sisyphean Lover

Dawn Terpstra

You are seldom handsome or elegant
after we've had a go at it,
daylight dries our ecstatic drips and dabs.

I breathe deep before caressing
your rough form, singing your
unvoiced self, no matter the rags
or finery tailored for your debut.

You've provoked this solo show,
keeping dreams and sleep from my bed
with your urgency. Your breath
hot on my neck when morning colors
the window. Your clever curiosity feeds
a mind hungry behind a windshield
driving dreamlike along a divided highway,
your amorphous face an idea for a destination.

Sometimes you're a bastard,
never holding me when I writhe with sobs,
or toweling me dry when I dive for words
lodged between mossy bricks in the soul's deep well.

When I see your eyes, I forgive you,
while seeking a synonym for *pain in the ass.*

I make you real in the quiet hours,
sculpt your form and substance
from the cool clay of choke and churn,
folding in the absent-ordinary,
truth-in-a-twist, mouth-music.

For days I fuss over you,
turning your face to new light,
brushing back lines, shaving stray words,
schooling your arms to open for others.

Yet sometimes, you win.

What audience exists for one so loved,
running barefoot into the tall grass?

HER DREAM

Hans Krueger

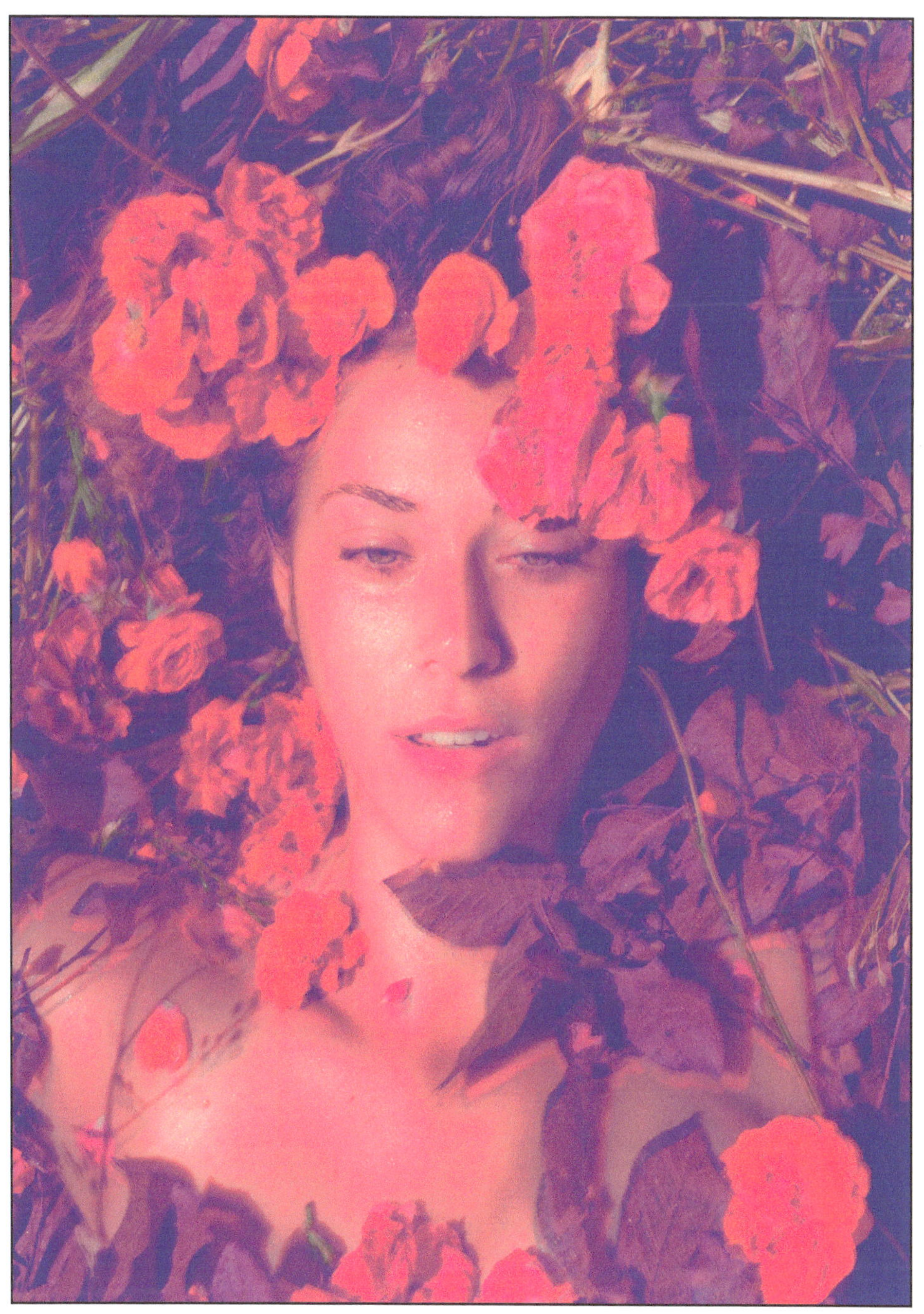

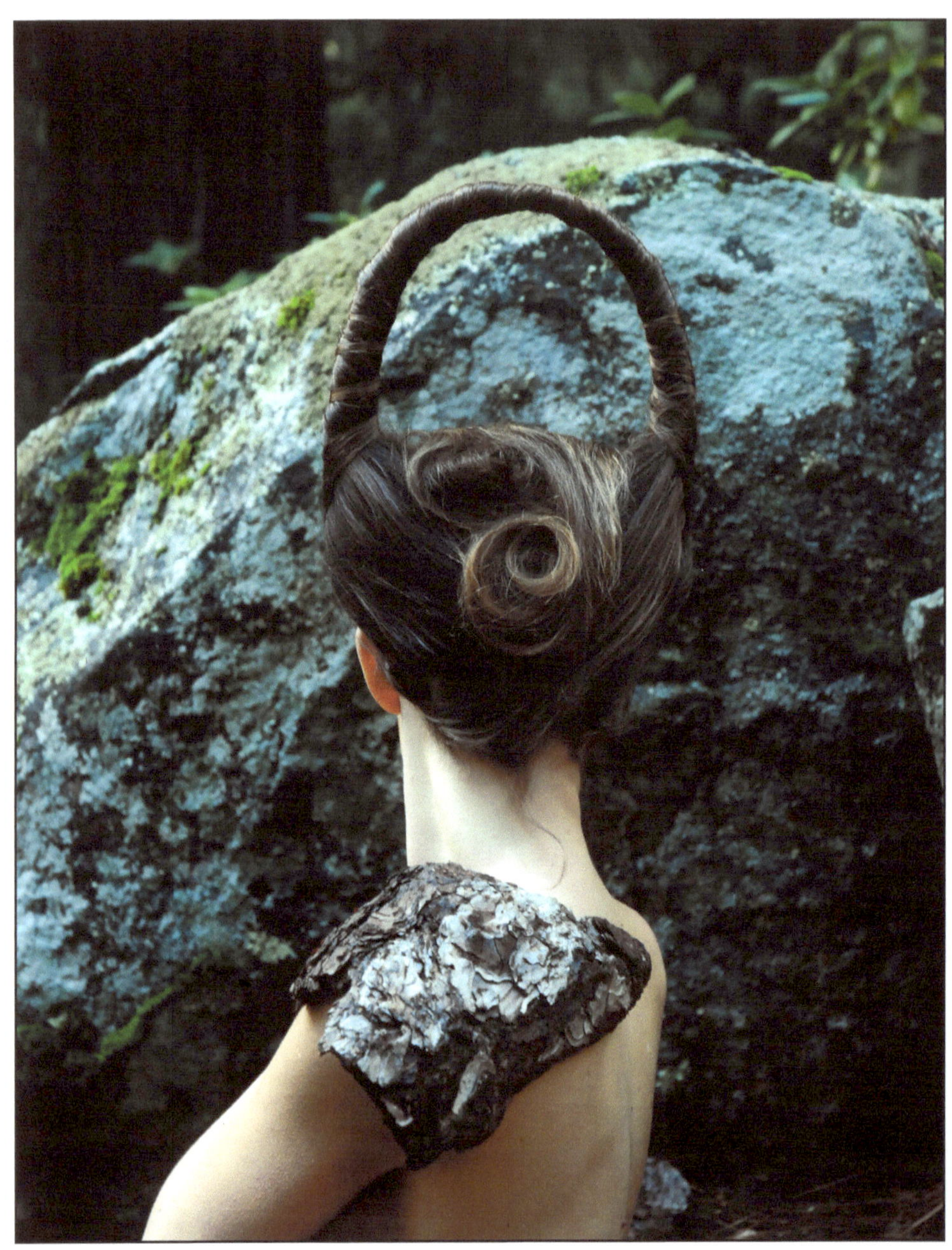

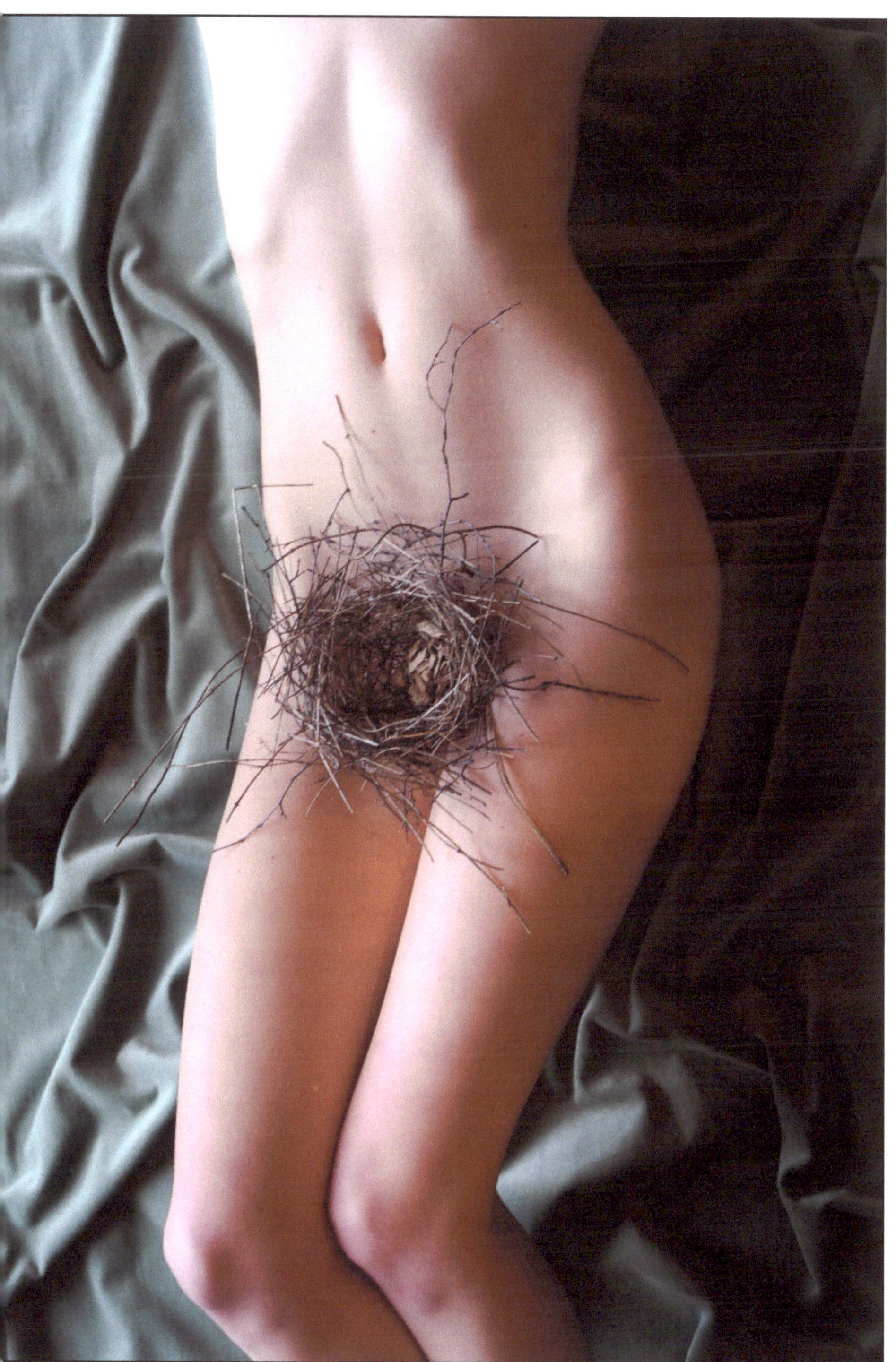

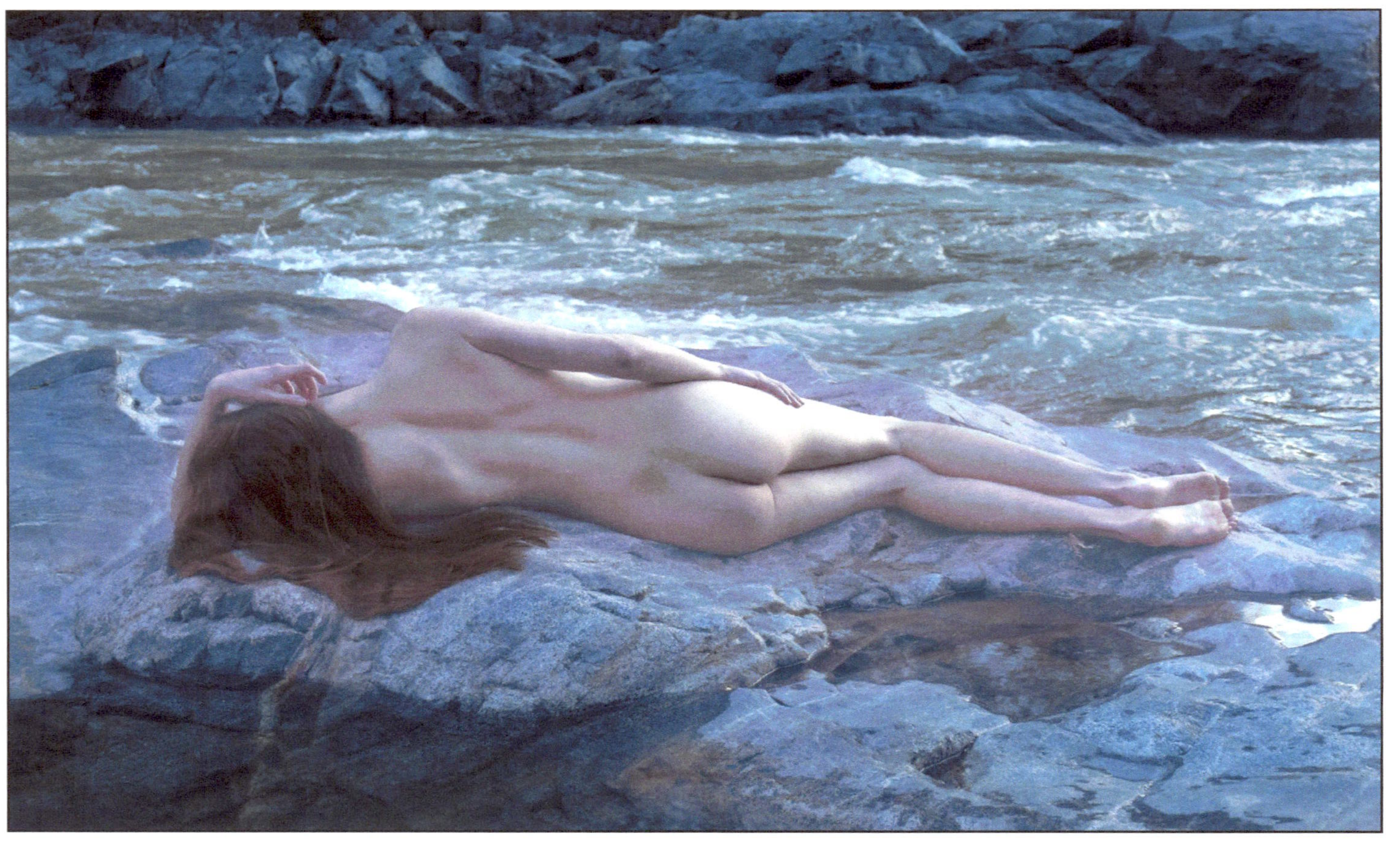

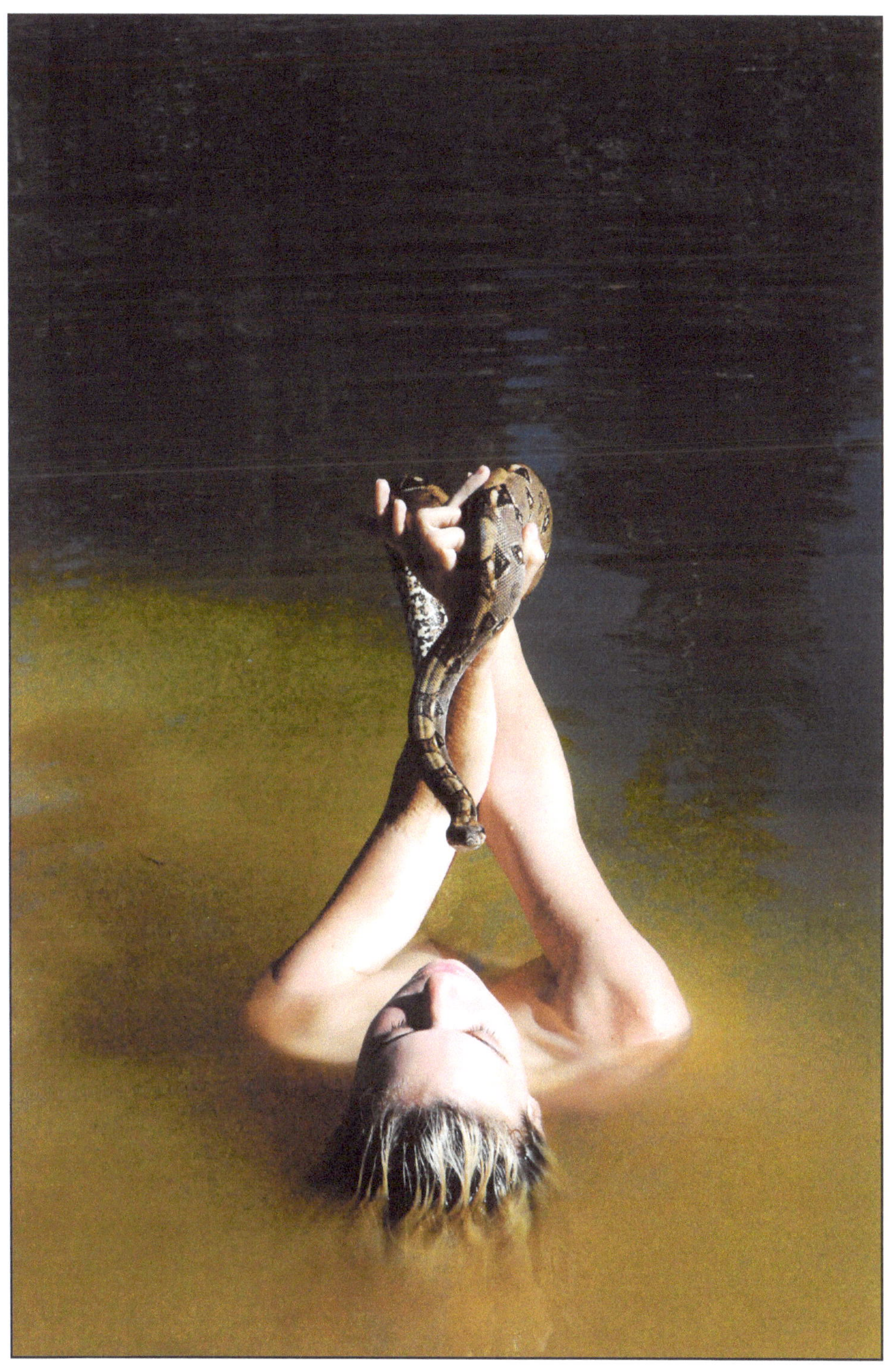

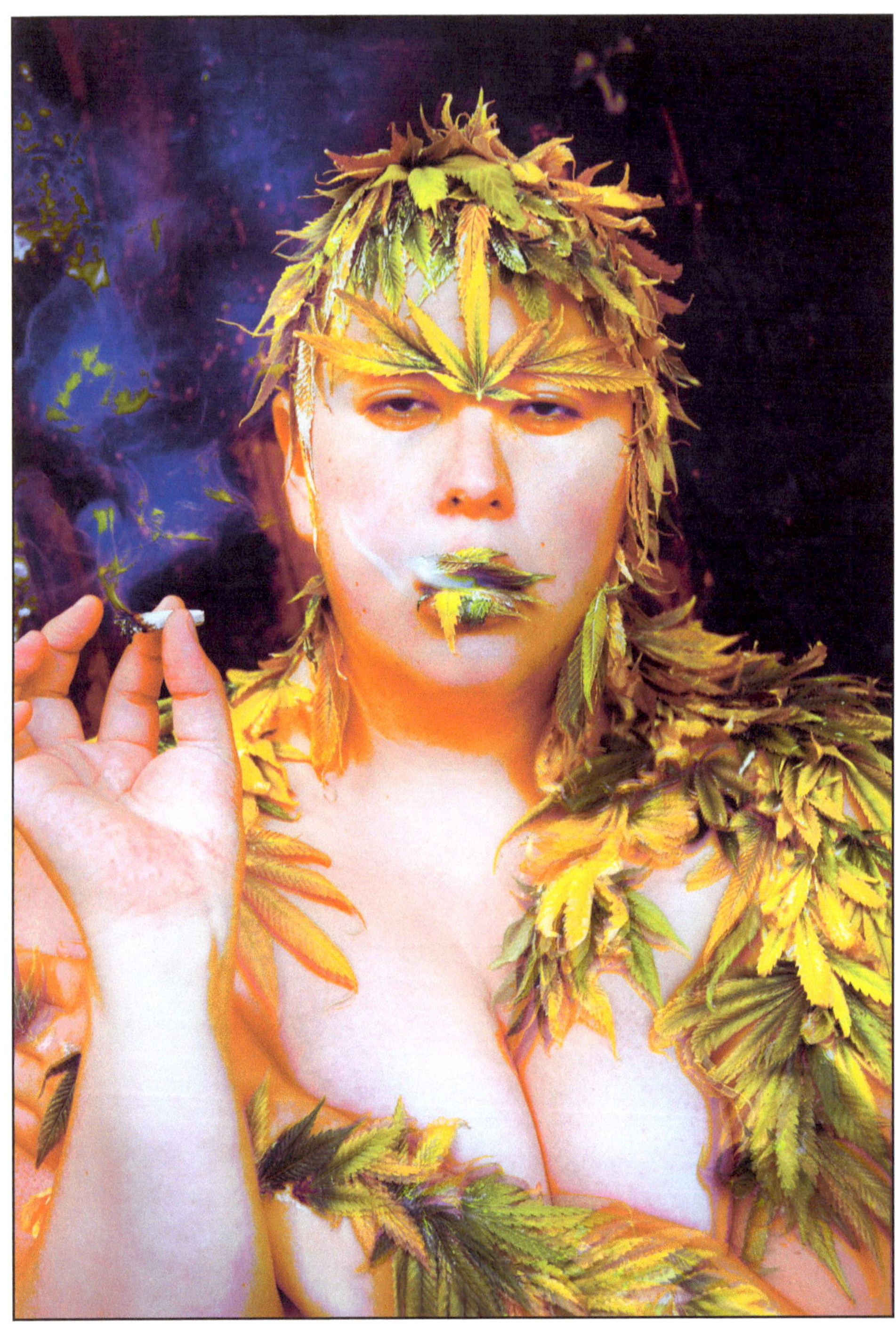

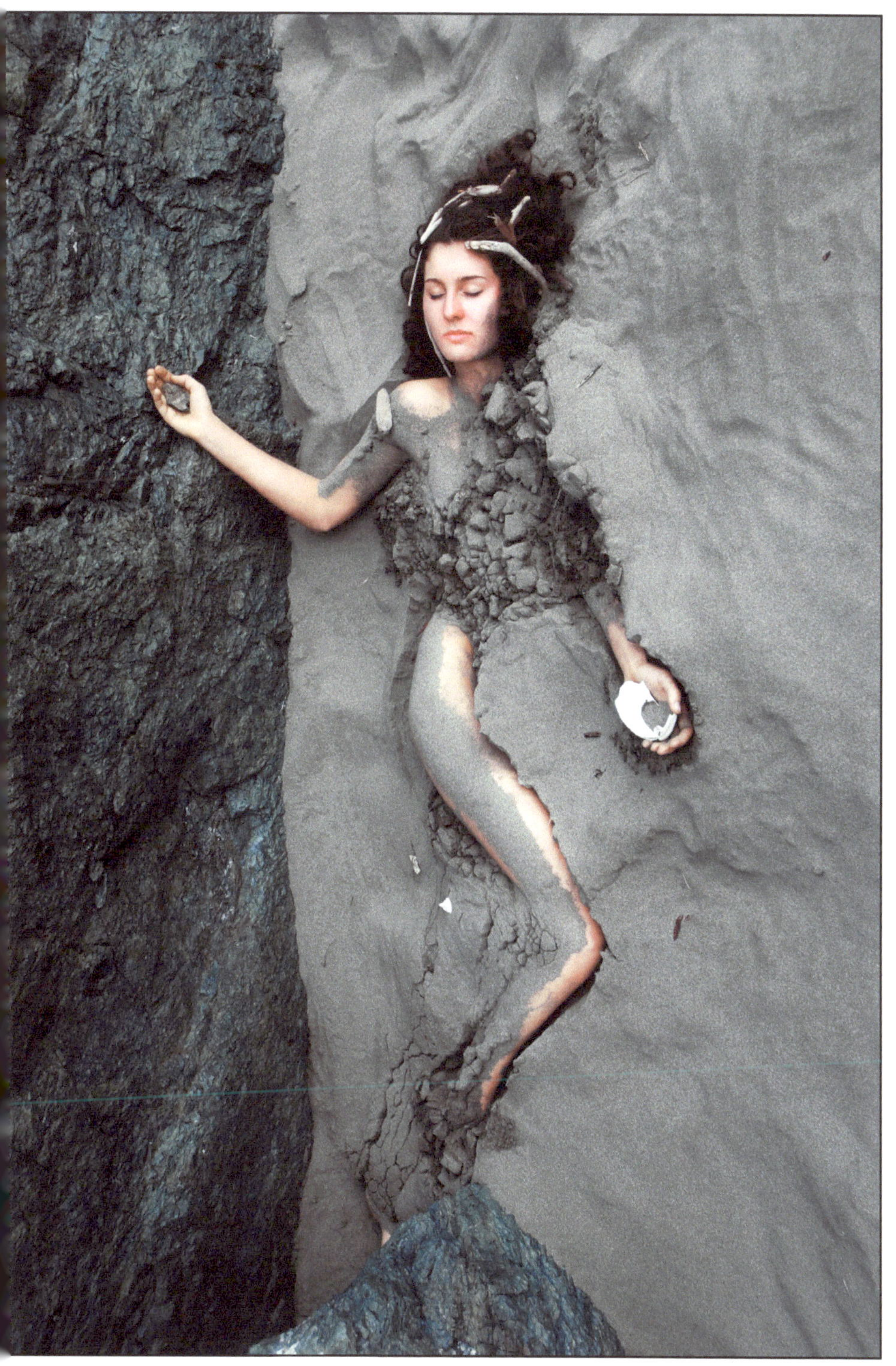

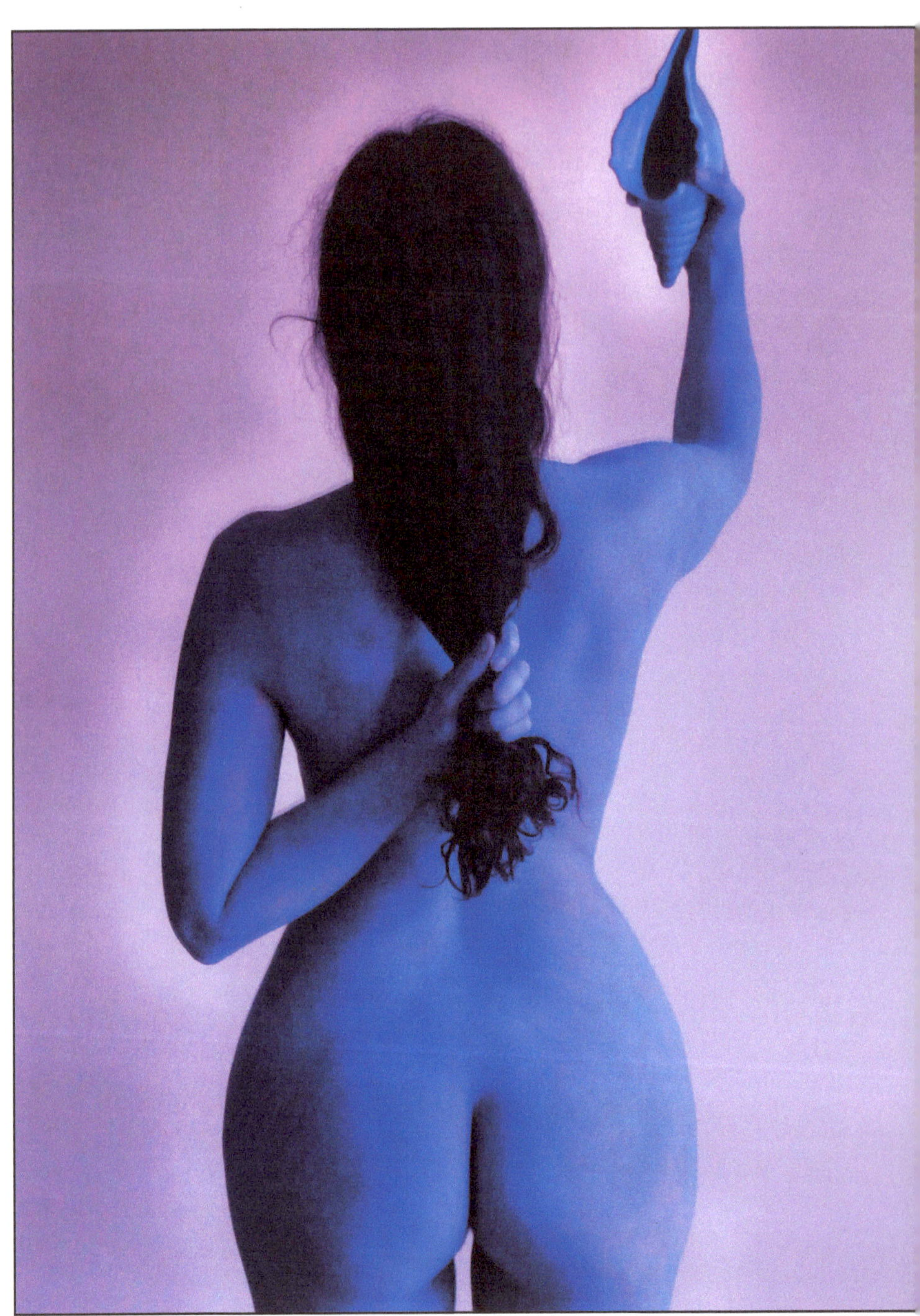

Double Sonnet

Julia Lattimer

They're walking through the park playing a po-
em in their head, can picture the place where the line
breaks on fracture, looking at the snowy hill
in the dark with their hands in their pockets and chewing a spear-
mint gum. Afraid of slipping, they shuffle boots
over the slick, step on ripples in the concrete path,
root-broken, even away from the trees. *A part-*
ner is one way of imagining what comes next,

they think, and then walk away from the thought
in the dark, past the tennis court's chain link fence;
its blotchy puddles of terrible ice like winter lakes
under the moony yellow street light. They've been
alone for a very long time. They turn
a corner and head toward the people street.

After so many former futures,
they know this park, can remember lying
next to an imaginary on the hill,
grass scratching through their T-shirt, the smell
of potential's shampoo bubbling up inside them
in the sun, buoyant, a crescent above the brim.

But now they're counting meter on their hands
in the dark. And the wind—*they can feel it!*—is worst
when they're walking out in the open without
gloves, following brownish footprints in the ice,
noticing their feet as smaller, their eyes
as brutal; when they'll be in this park this park
for a very long time, and their body carries
cold like sound rattles in an empty glass.

Candor

Kate Cumiskey

Write a poem about the dried flowers hanging from the curtain rod.
Write your mother, your sister's ex-boyfriend, your hemorrhoids.
Write one honest politician you've shaken hands with; then
write Trump. Write about the eleventh grade American
History teacher who wanted to fuck you.

Write the zoology teacher who raped your best friend. Write
developers from Miami and New York raping the estuary.
Write your history; write that fear at 2 a.m. the night
your son overdosed. Write tile beneath your knees.
Write rats in the kitchen, raccoons in the roof, your dog
over the fence, gone all night.

Write the phone not ringing. Write your first fuck,
your latest one. Write the student you wish would just shut
the fuck up and write one paragraph. Write the one who scares you
& the girl you wish somebody would say hello to. Write the gay boy
your heart breaks for. Write punching the wall of your bedroom at
sixteen. Write solutions you dream before they slip into the fetid
air. Write a poem.

LIMINAL ANIMISM: THE MASKS OF VENICE

Linda Briskin

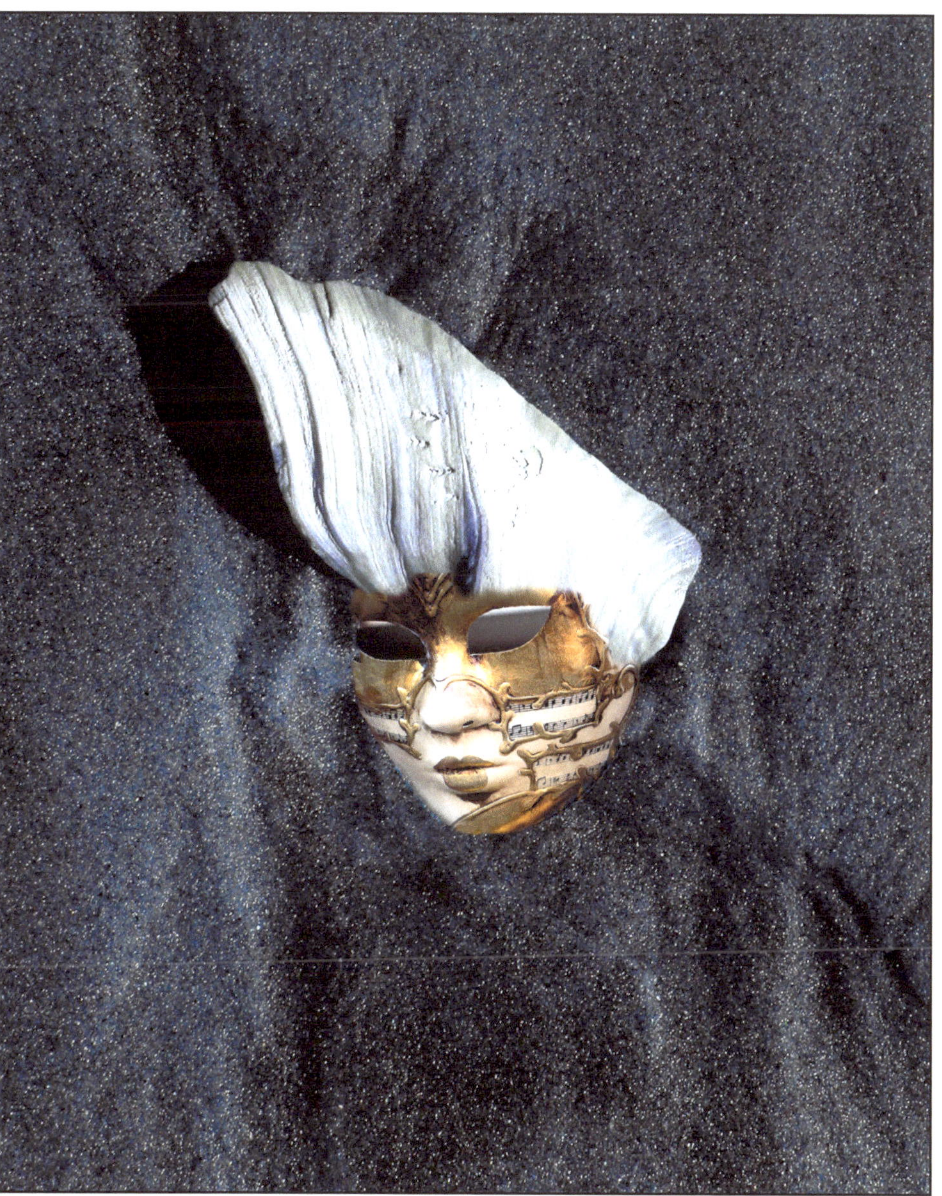

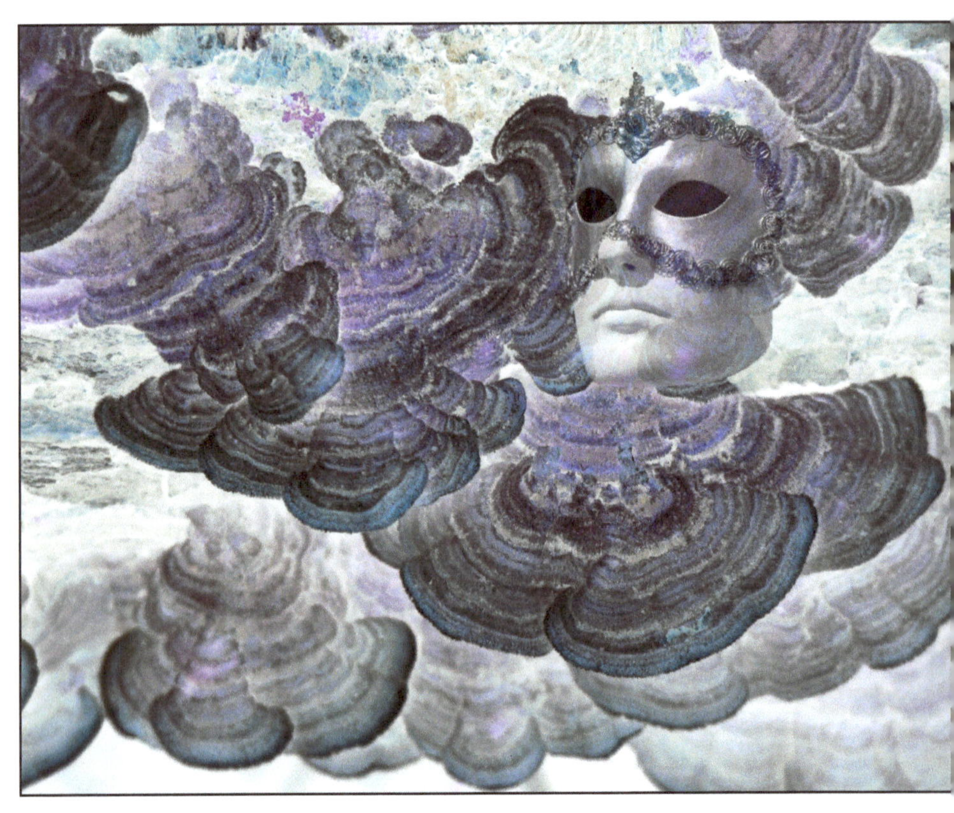

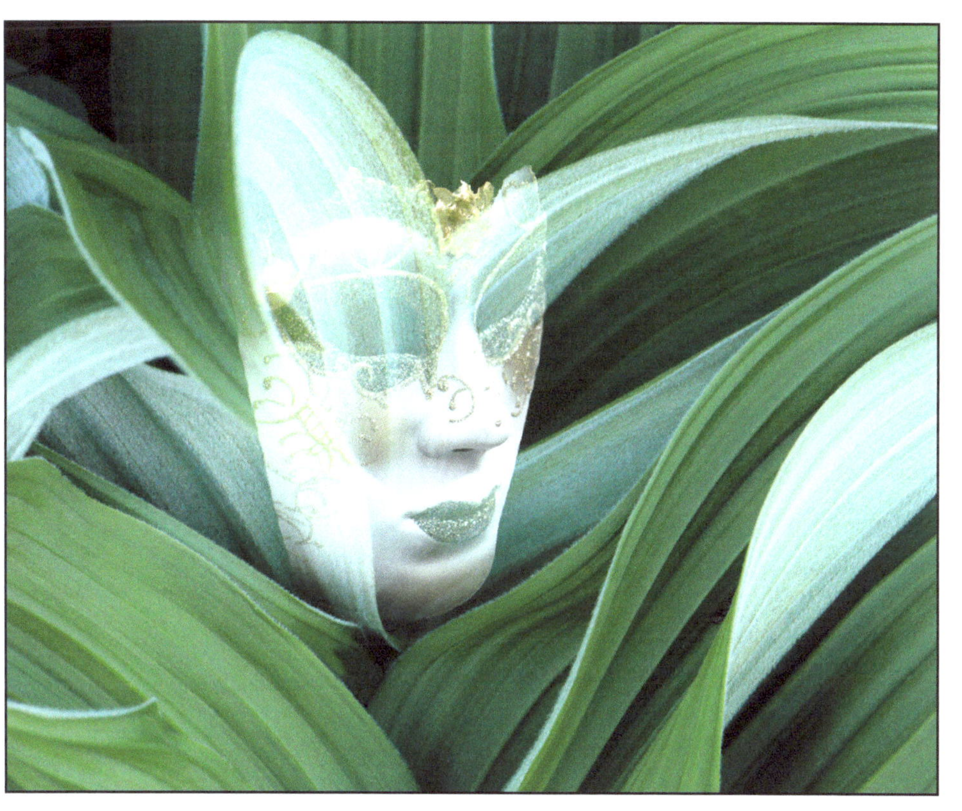

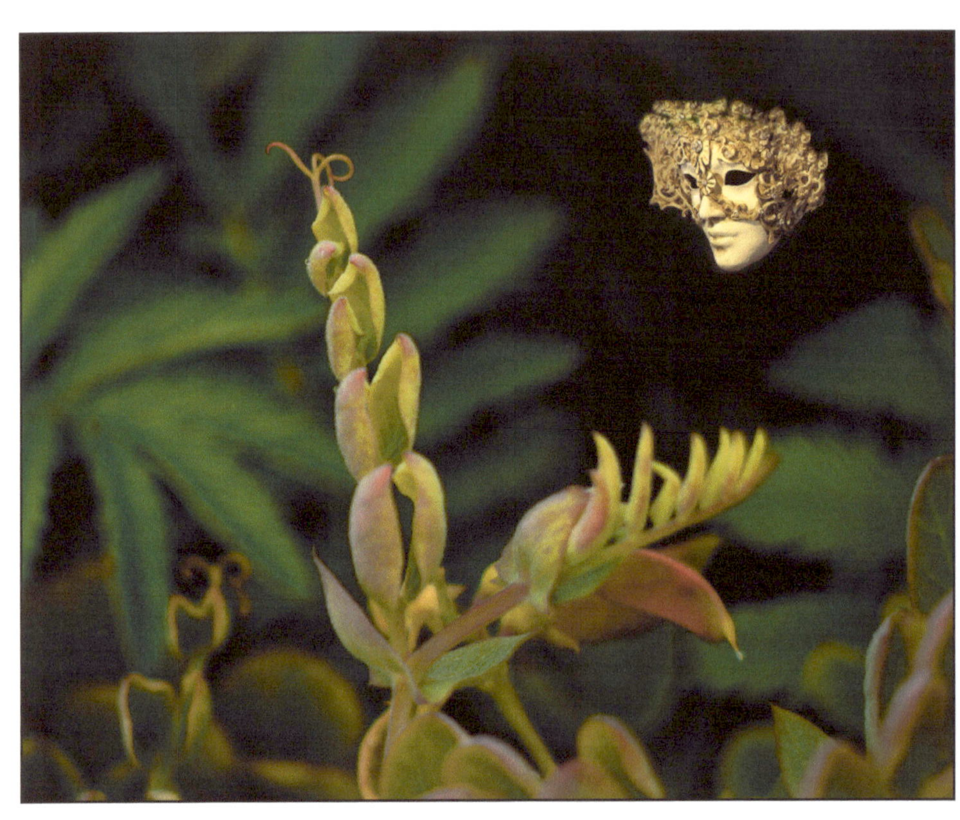

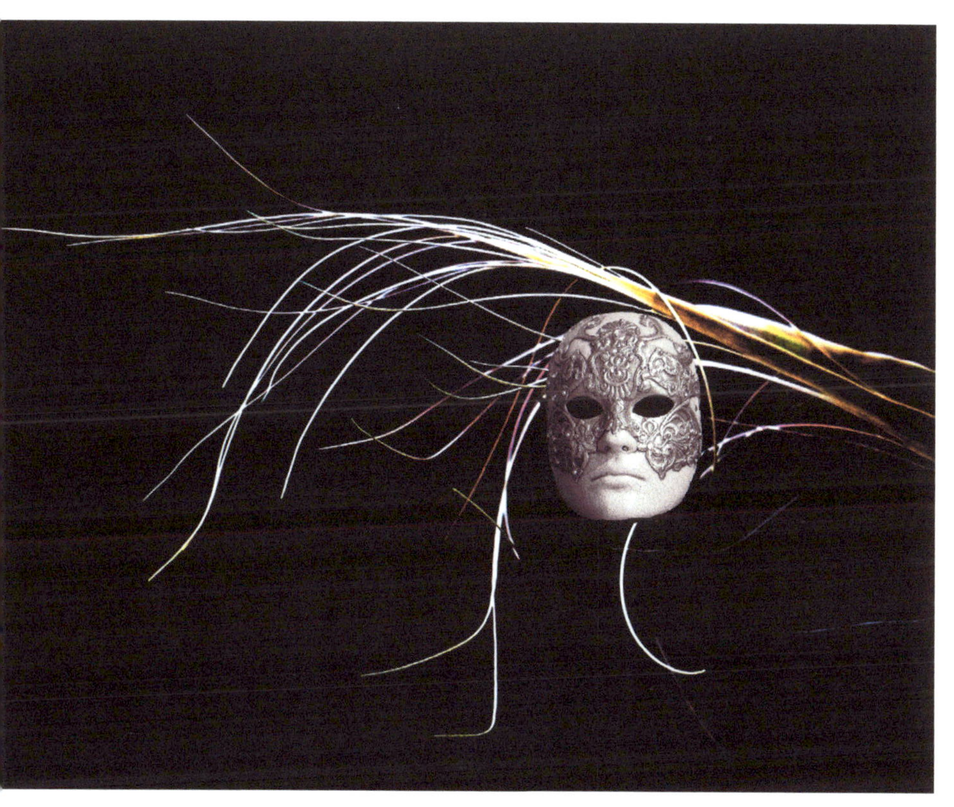

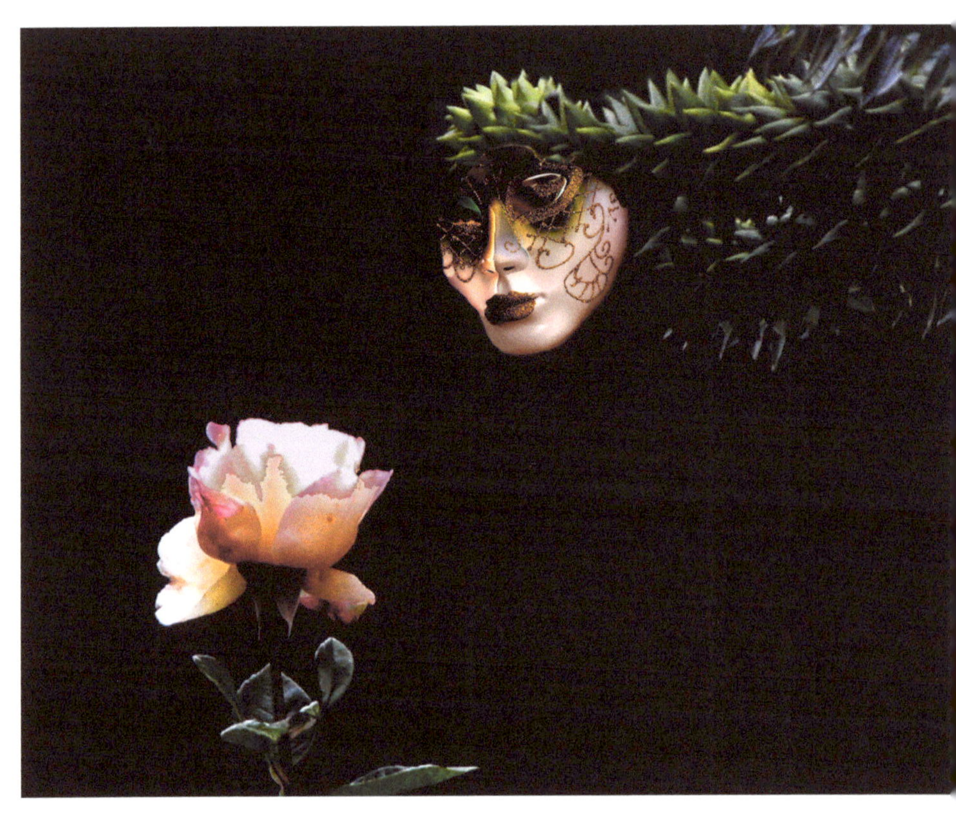

I Have A Problem

Kirk Boys

I recently began trying to practice Mindfulness. I'm taking a class. If you don't know, Mindfulness is the art of living life in the moment, the here and now so to speak. That involves forgetting the past and not fretting about the future and I have to admit that I am not so good at that. Apparently, I have a lot to mull over.

People ask, "Why would you do something like that?"

I tell them, "I am trying to become a better, healthier, happier person."

The question is how does staring at a ladybug crawl across a leaf or meditating on the shape of a cloud or taking the time to really enjoy a cup of coffee make me a better, happier, healthier person? Living in the moment takes "me-time" and that seems sort of selfish if you want to know the truth. If I were a good person I wouldn't be in my own head, I would be trying to help other people's heads. When I say others, I mean people who are struggling: so, your poor people, your sick people, your immigrants, your homeless, your mentally ill, your Evangelicals.

I was thinking the other day that to be a better person, I should be volunteering more, but even that has its downside. You can come across as self-righteous. That doesn't make me a better person. Maybe the answer is to donate money. Writing a check is my go-to against feeling guilty, but writing a check is a cop-out, everybody knows that.

You know how they say, "You can't help someone else if you can't help yourself." It's the type of thing you'd hear from a counselor or a psychiatrist to make you feel better about being selfish. They might even give you a prescription for some medication that would help you to not feel anything.

It's all too confusing. What should I be doing to be a happier, healthier and better person. If I made a list it might make me less anxious and I could really get into that cup of coffee or watch that cloud form.

I feel guilty about my white privilege. I blame my parents for most everything since they've both passed on and can't defend themselves. In addition, I've gained a few pounds and I should be working out more and watching what I eat more closely, not too much salt, fat or corn syrup. There's a chance I could be gluten intolerant, but I have no way of knowing since I haven't had a physical in some time. I'll just research it on Web MD.

Then there's my drinking. My wife says, "You need to cut back." She tells me, "You might have a drinking problem." And that could be the reason I don't like what I see in the mirror after my shower no matter how much I suck in my gut or flex my muscle. Which reminds me I should be putting sunscreen on before I go out in the sun as skin cancer is everywhere. People are catching it like crazy.

On the spiritual front I haven't gone to church since Easter and even then we left mass early to make it to brunch on time. I guess I need to put that on the To-Do list along with the five grandkids whom I'm told aren't getting enough of my time. My daughter said just the other day, "Dad you need to spend more time with the kids."

I need to take the dog for a walk every day. Not to mention there's plenty to get done around the house, dusting, windows and weeding in the yard and speaking of the house, it's time my wife and I sell and move into the city and buy an electric car. My wife said just the other day, "Why are we living in the suburbs. We don't have any kids in school or little league or dance class. We don't belong in the suburbs anymore our kids are grown and gone. We should be in the city closer to real bookstores and independent movie houses and gourmet restaurants and poetry readings. We need to live somewhere we can walk to things before we can't walk anymore."

And I said to her, "I like that Home Depot is so close and Costco and Fred Meyer and Red Robin and MacDonald's and Burger King are all just a short drive away. What if I park at the far end of the lot and just walk more?"

And she says to me, "You've got a problem."

I should also be getting involved in politics, doorbelling and organizing and such. That deserves my time too. Which brings me to sleep. I need more sleep. "You're sleep deprived" my wife says.

"It takes me one second to fall asleep," I tell her. I'm very proud of that statistic.

"That's a problem," she says. "You should determine if you have Sleep Apnea." It's as bad as skin cancer. People are catching it like crazy too.

It's a good thing I'm retired.

My tennis game is crumbling. I used to be really good, but now I need lessons and practice time but my knees ache. There is also the matter of making some new friendships, especially if I plan on living past 70. Friendship extends life, I read that somewhere. I spend too much time on my phone and watching golf on TV and I need to work on my flexibility which means signing up for a yoga class I guess.

It's a lot to consider.

"It needs to happen," my wife tells me.

I have too much on my plate to worry about moments or ladybugs or the way the wind rustles the leaves or shadows dance on a sunny day or how my body feels when I take a breath. I need to help other people to feel good about myself. I wish there was a pill for all of that because I'm burning time just thinking about all the stuff I need to do.

Or, maybe I should forget about all that stuff and watch a ladybug, see how it handles itself. Maybe I'd learn something.

City Planning Pantoum
Josh Feit

The time it takes your lungs to learn Ravi Shankar's Midnight raga is the same
as it takes your apartment to turn Macadamias into honey. The sweetest story I ever
heard was about the boyfriend who greeted his girlfriend at the station platform dressed
in her clothes. Their future was doomed. The sidewalk is made of broken verse.

The sweetest story I ever heard was about the girlfriend who hung a hammock of stars
beneath the sidewalk canopy for her blind boyfriend. Midnight-to-Six
is the metric city planners should use to see the sidewalk. The wind is made of
apartment buildings. Separatist metrics cannot blur this artless notion that shelter is
somehow bad for the neighborhood.

Midnight-to-Six is the metric city planners should use when they dress up in furs and
platform shoes to survey the district. A verse from Bo Diddley's *Pretty Thing* is a
rendering of Ravi Shankar's evening raga. The artless notion that additional housing is
bad follows the artless notion that shelter requires mitigation. Apartment buildings are
made of our returns from the station.

Greetings, I'm on the art committee for the skate park. The time it takes to turn verses
into resources is the same as to dress up in fur & silk glamour. The sidewalk is made of
stories about boyfriends & girlfriends. Like the one about the future, when Midnight asks
the canopy: Do your lungs have a favorite song, at this late hour?

Second Amendment Blues

Art Bell

A recent letter to NRA Members from Wayne LaPierre, Executive Vice President

Hi there,

Okay, so this latest mass shooting may look distressing to some of you out there and I feel your concern. But worry not, this massacre, like all the others, will fade from the hearts and minds of most Americans as quickly as the sharp retort from an AR-15 in a gymnasium during a high school basketball game. Which is to say (for those of you who are a little slow on metaphors), quickly.

I do want to point out to you that this may be an apt moment for our organization to redefine our mission. We've called ourselves the NRA (the National Rifle Association, again for the slower members in our group) for many years now. But of course, the ability to own and use rifles in any way we see fit is only a part of what we are protecting for red-blooded Americans. We've moved on to semi-automatic weapons of all kinds, including our beloved handguns with monster ammo clips. And look at how successful we've been at convincing America that these are ever so useful in "hunting," which is one important reason we need more of them.

And, thanks to lobbying by some of our deafer members, we are this close to making gun silencers legal. I SAID, "THANKS TO SOME OF OUR DEAFER MEMBERS"... Just joking. With silencers legally available for purchase, ear protection will become completely unnecessary! No more innocent bystanders going temporarily deaf around gunshots. See? The NRA does have a heart!

Now is the time to go to the next level.

First, let me suggest that hand grenades be added to the weapons guaranteed by the constitution. A "well-armed militia" implies, I believe, the best possible arms available. Just imagine how effective a grenade would be on the hunt: why take out a single elk buck when with one well-aimed grenade you can take out the whole herd? When we start coming home from the hunt with tons of elk meat for our friends and families, I think everyone will see the wisdom in this. And (bonus!) grenades are concealable weapons which puts them in the same category as the handguns that people are able to take to work, to college, to national parks. So I hereby recommend that we add grenades to the list of protected weaponry in the US. My next letter to you will provide sufficient details for those of you wishing to know what kind, how big, where to buy, cost, etc.

Next, I think surface-to-air missiles would be very useful in bird hunting, especially for those really giant majestic looking birds. How great would it be to see a bald eagle blown to smithereens by a heat-seeking missile? Boom! Wait, are bald eagles still a protected species? Okay, Peregrine falcons then. Let's be careful with this one, because, of course, if any of these SAM's fell into the hands of those crazy guys who like to take out people (wait, aren't people a protected species? Smiley Face!), we could put some airliners at risk. But look, as we've always said, if people were adequately armed, there would be fewer deaths from these things. (I'm still looking for how that argument might apply to blowing up planes even if everyone in the plane was armed to the teeth, but we have people in our organization smarter than me who are good at this. Well, nearly as smart as me.)

Last, I'd like to invite our members to write in with additional suggestions for growing our hunting arsenal. No bad ideas. Wait, nuclear stuff is a bad idea since this can be dangerous to the guy using the nuclear weapons and I don't think we're capable of providing training on them. Yet. For now, let's leave them out.

While it is truly sad that some folks died in what may have been a preventable massacre, let's look for the silver lining here, okay? No long faces, this is going to work out great for us!

Yours in shooting big weaponry as often as possible,

Wayne LaPierre,
Executive Vice President
National Rifle Association

Cannoli Friday

Jesse Stein

When Manchego Reginald Beemster rose to power, his first act as President was to ban all cheese consumption. It was an Executive Order, and there was nothing the Dairy Lobby could do. The Dairy Lobby was old monied and aristocratic, monocled with hidden illegitimate children. Certainly this bastion of influence, solidified and compounded across many generations, would have at least ushered some variation of a compromise; a rationing campaign perhaps. But no, they were deflated and dismantled by Mr. Beemster, who as a sentient wheel of cheese in a $3000 suit, found our human addiction to his flesh untoward. Violation of this decree meant certain death, death by grating in fact, and so the American public felt their once cherished independence evaporate, though collectively they were less gassy.

President Beemster surrounded himself with lactose-intolerant sycophants, men and women who he knew wouldn't objectify or patronize him as a consumable. He soon found that all of his ideas were quite brilliant, no matter the audacity or impracticality. It started off small, like moving the White House to a cave in the outskirts of Madison, Wisconsin, where the temperature kept him fresh. But as he hoarded more and more of those allergic to dairy, and as he watched them tirelessly appease his every whim, he soon understood that he was, indeed, special. Not only special, but better. Someone deserving of more than what he had. So naturally, the next step was world domination. Mexico crumbled like a moldy Stilton. Beemster was sending a message to the world, and it was curdling. He paid particular devastating attention to the regions of Oaxaca and Chihuahua, in an endless series of night-bombings by his new G-oUD4 stealth bombers. From there he moved south with little resistance, offering the countries that joined him willingly clemency, given of course, that they gave up their dairy consumption.

This is not to say that the rest of the world was idle, that they were able to envision a reality *sans* dairy. Europe in particular, became a hotbed of Pro-Dairy propaganda, plastering their brick-lined streets and gothic city squares with nutritional value tables. Leaders gave uplifting and impassioned speeches on the benefits of calcium and vitamin D. In an unprecedented move, England, France, and Italy, who have historically clashed over religion, empire, and cuisine for thousands of years, forged a new alliance, *Fromage Ou Mort* (FOM). Thousands of ships carrying Cheesemongers and Sheep Herders poured into their docks, volunteers for the FOM International Defenders of Cheese (FOMIDC) swelled, and soon, they had a force that could stand up to Beemster's Plug the Udder Brigade (PUB).

Beemster was swollen and sweating and filled with rage at these Old-World upstarts. He saw himself as a savior, one who was halting the industrialized genocide of his people, and he swore to make the insatiable gluttons pay for their violent appetites. President Beemster wasted no time in rallying his troops for his next move, the annihilation of France. He saw this backwards country as the center of the revolutionary movement, and therefore vowed to spit on the ruins of *Notre Dame* before Christmas. The stage was set, the pieces were moving, it would be a World War to end all World Wars.

The fighting lasted months. *Cannoli Friday*, the bloodiest battle in all of human history, claimed the lives of over 4 million Defenders of Cheese, and just under 7 Million Plug the Udders. The fearsome and dashing Frenchman, Général Par Majean, was able to use the secret and oft-forgotten underground caverns that stretch underneath all of Europe to his advantage, and turned the tide of the battle, routing Beemster's forces.

When the dust settled, it was clear that Beemster wasn't the demi-god that he presented himself as. He was fallible, he was after all, a wheel of cheese. Discord blemished throughout his fast-won empire, even his own cabinet members, those who trusted and worshipped him the most, began to whisper when he left the room. President Manchego Reginald Beemster fled the Old-World and attempted to regroup in his cave outside of Madison. The FOD sent agents into America, to sow discord and foster a coup, CIA style. A Ten-Story high Cheese Grater was raised, and marched to Madison, where Beemster sat, drunk on wine with a pistol pressed into his temple. He couldn't grasp what all of the fuss was about. What was it about cheese that humans loved so much? Why were they willing to die over glorified mold? Could it really taste that good?

The mob bled into his cave, drooling and lusting after his innards. But all they could find was a $3000 dollar suit, dusted with crumbs of cheese, soaked in red wine. Further investigation revealed a single line, hastily scratched into the cave wall.

Mon vie, c'est dommage. Parce-que maintenant, je veux seulement manger fromage

Subway Drifter

Photography by George L Stein
Poetry by Shimon Moore

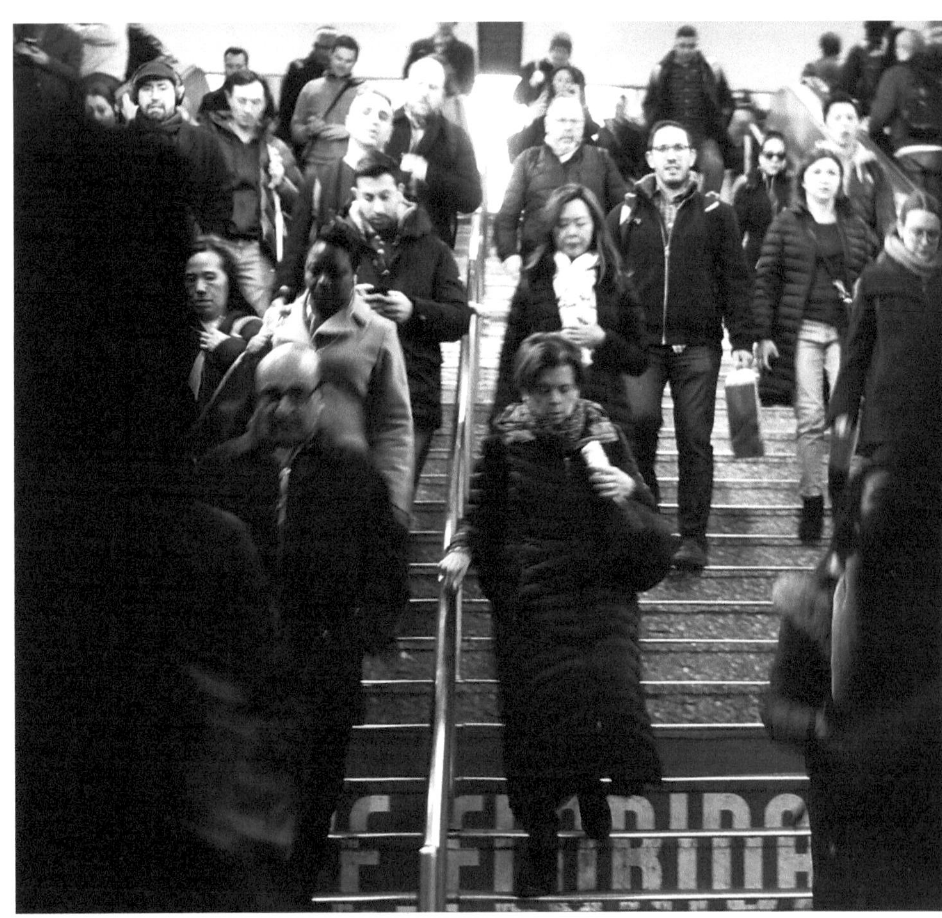

Do you see me?

Your eyes divert with the clumsiness
of a compass too polite for pointing to
true south. This drifter, too low in the stratosphere
of economic bodies to space direction.
The lines your eyes sketch around my form,
divert into white space,
into a silence of held breaths and murmurs.
Lord, it almost proves you do

See me

I am not cold yet in your black coffin coats,
a trash bagged body in Charon's boat
of social death.

See me

No wallet to prick the sieves of thieves,
or beauty to gut for a low-scum rider. But
my brother said my name so long ago
I can hear it like a haunt,
like my own blood's cry
muffled in a ground raped dry
clashing against the eardrums
of a raging God polishing his scales.

See me

Without the soul connection that comes
In the glance of a weary eye,
I am erased. You're all a blurr
of gray ghosts rippling down
the shiver Styx, these stairs

See me

If gravity could make me rise
In your eyes
I would make you

See me.

Perhaps you're the ones undead.
Not spirit, but blistered shell,
used up like a bullet shot once and reloaded.
And I, the warm rushing blood you gush through,
have more substance than the light above
could cast on this subway drifter.

In Order Of Appearance:

Annie has been featured in Hobart, A VELVET GIANT, and has upcoming publications in great weather for MEDIA and Gigantic Sequins. She likes to wear lipstick and spin in circles.

Melinda Winograd lives in Dallas, Texas where she works as an Intelligence Consultant. She studied poetry at the University of North Texas, and currently studies fiction writing at Southern New Hampshire University. Her work has been featured in The Tulane Review.

Linda Eve Diamond is an award-winning poet whose creative works have been published by "Grey Sparrow Journal," "Gravel," "Your Daily Poem," "Encore: Prize Poems 2018," and others. Find her poetry collections, selected poems, flash fiction, and photographs at www.LindaEveDiamond.com.

Charise M. Hoge is a dance/movement therapist, performing artist, and writer. Her work in arts and healing has brought wellness programs into hospitals, counseling centers, museums, and businesses. Her poetry is featured in various journals as well as her chapbook Striking Light from Ashes and the book Next Line, Please: Prompts to Inspire Poets and Writers. Charise continues to dance professionally in collaboration with choreographers in the D.C. area, and faithfully blogs at mixandmosspoetry.com.

Robert Grant is a poet-screenwriter whose poems have appeared in DASH Literary Journal, Mudfish, The Esthetic Apostle, etc.—as well as on numerous unsolicited postcards to family and friends. Recently, he helped a retired US Air Force colonel write his memoir. He is currently at work on a family drama (screenplay). San Francisco based artist,

Gwen Pryor (b.1989) uses drones to capture new perspectives and compositions for her oil paintings. Her paintings make the viewer reconsider familiar seascapes by showing them an aerial and abstracted perspective. She is passionate about oceanic preservation and hopes her art will inspire viewers to protect the environment. She studied art at Skidmore College.

Nick Lopez is a Marine Corps veteran, who served from 2005-20013 and is currently a coordinator for veteran programs at the Veterans of Foreign Wars National Headquarters in Kansas City, MO. He also volunteers on the board of the Kansas City Veterans Writing Team based out of Kansas City area and was most recently published in Veteran's Voices and Haiku Journal.

Ian Randall Wilson's fiction and and poetry have appeared in a number of literary journals including the North American Review, The Gettysburg Review and Alaska Quarterly Review. A short story collection, Hunger and Other Stories, was published by Hollyridge Press. His first poetry collection, Ruthless Heaven, was published by Finishing Line Press. He has an MFA in Poetry and in Fiction from Warren Wilson College, and is on the fiction faculty at the UCLA Extension. By day he works at Sony Pictures in Los Angeles.

Fesuk, a Massachusetts native, teaches English in Marietta, Georgia and has earned degrees from the University of Georgia, Agnes Scott College, Kennesaw State University, and, most recently, the Etowah Valley MFA from Reinhardt University; her current full-length manuscript, Mamabird, has recently been accepted for publication. Fesuk studied English and Creative Writing in the doctoral program at Georgia State University and was a Georgia Author of the Year Award nominee for her chapbook If Not an Apple (La Vita Poetica Press). She worked as Poet in Residence at The Walker School, served as Creative Writer in Residence at the Kennesaw Mountain Writing Project, and published poems that can be found in more than thirty journals including Five Points, Poet Lore, The Pedestal, Slant, Atlanta Review, and Wicked Alice.

Ashley Shelby is the author of South Pole Station: A Novel and Red River Rising: The Anatomy of a Flood and the Survival of an American City. Her novel was one of Shelf Awareness' Best Novels of 2017, a New York Times Book Review Editors' Choice, and one of Millions' Most Anticipated Books of 2017. More information can be found at www.ashleyshelby.com.

Zoe Canner's writing has appeared in The Laurel Review, Arcturus of the Chicago Review of Books, Naugatuck River Review, SUSAN / The Journal, Maudlin House, Occulum, Pouch, Matter, Chaleur Magazine, Nailed Magazine, Indolent Books' What Rough Beast, and elsewhere. She lives in Los Angeles where she indulges in hilly walks at dusk when the night-blooming jasmine is at its peak fragrance. www.zoecanner.com

Tiffany Promise's writing has previously been published in Black Clock, Blanket Sea, and Gingerbread House. She received her MFA from CalArts a few years ago, and is currently living in Victoria, B.C. while figuring out how to juggle motherhood and writing. She just completed her first novel.

Tara Cronin is an artist working in various mediums, focusing on photography, installation and book arts. She received her MFA from the ICP-Bard Program in New York. She received her BA in Writing at New School University. While Tara battled hospitalizations and mental illness during her undergraduate work, her healing process veered her toward combining photography, writing, and artmaking in response. This project highlights the history of mischaracterizing LGBT members as mentally ill, psychotic, unstable, unhinged, and "crazy" so that society can remember what this community had to struggle through to reach their current status of equality.

Nicole Rose Schoonbrood has been acknowledged for her jarring language and outlandish imagery by the awarded poets Joseph Lease and Heather Gibbons. In the process of completing a Bachelor's Degree in Creative Writing at SFSU, Nicole has discovered the driving grotesquery and rawness of her work. Nicole finds the exploration of self, the interaction between experience and consciousness, as well as the eternal unknown to be the core performers of her imagination.

Kristin Snow is a Colorado writer and artist. She has studied poetry with Phillis Levin at the 92nd St. Y, as well as with Black Mountain poet Edward Dorn. Her writing is influenced by the Black Mountain Poets - particularly the projectivist verse style exemplified by Robert Creeley. She holds a Master's degree in Creative Writing from the University of Denver, and an undergraduate degree in English Literature from Lafayette College. She has won numerous awards for her work including two awards for poetry from the Denver Women's Press Club; a Colorado State Poetry Award, a California State Poetry Award and a NJ State Poetry Award. She has also been recognized for commercial writing with an Emmy Award.

Marina Hatsopoulos's writing has been published in Antioch Review, Bellevue Literary, Crab Orchard Review, F(r)iction by Tethered by Letters, The Write Launch, Pooled Ink: NCW Contest Winners, and numerous other literary journals. Marina's work has been winner or finalist in the F(r)iction Short Story Contest, the PNWA literary contest, the Jack Dyer Fiction Prize, the Prolitzer Prize and the Glimmer Train Short Story Award for new writers. Marina was Co-Founder/CEO of Z Corporation, an early leader in 3D printing out of MIT.

Dawn Sly-Terpstra is pursuing her lifelong passion of writing poetry, short fiction and non-fiction. She values the mentorship she finds from the poets of Omega and Sisyphean Writers. With masters degrees in both anthropology and family studies, she enjoys discoveries of culture, magic, and family wherever she travels. With deep roots in her home state of Iowa, she is inspired by connections to the natural world. Her work appears in Lyrical Iowa, Haiku Journal and in the upcoming edition of Cathexis Northwest Press. She has spent a career in communications and marketing and currently leads a corporate communications team.

Hans Krueger works in the medium of photography but also constructs the sets and designs the make up and hair his friends featured in his art. His work reflects the relationship between humans and their connection to the plant and animal kingdom.

Julia Lattimer is the Editor-in-chief of Breakwater Review. They were most recently named Editor's Choice in the 2019 Sandy Crimmons National Prize for Poetry and run a monthly queer reading series in Boston MA.

Kate Cumiskey is a graduate of the MFA program (poetry) at UNCW. She has a nonfiction book, Surfing in New Smyrna Beach, in its second run at Arcadia Press; another, University of Central Florida Through Time (Fonthill Media, London 2015); and Yonder, a book of poetry, from Silent e Publishing. Her work appears in Crazyhorse, Beloit Poetry Journal, Paterson Literary Review, Blood Orange Review and other lit mags.

Linda Briskin is a fine art photographer with ever-shifting photographic enthusiasms: light, lines, shadows, and the play of figure-ground; the juxtaposition of objects and reflections; the ambiguities in what we choose to see; and the permeability between the remembered and the imagined. Photo-collage is often used to construct unique and painterly images layered with nuance and narrative which both embrace and displace the original images. Her focus is less on capturing images than imagining and inventing them. Such an approach is fictive rather than representational.
In 2018, Briskin was selected for The New Feminist Gaze at Simeon Den Gallery in California. Her photograph 'Motorcycle Women' was published in Best of Photography 2018 by Photographers Forum. Recently in Toronto, she had a solo show at Helen & Hildegard Apothecary as part of the Junction Contact Festival, a window installation at Cutler & Gross, and participated in numerous group shows including Spectra at Gallery 1313 during the Contact Photography Festival. Upcoming are 'This is not a shoe store', a window installation at Rapp Optical, and 'Luminous', a group show of ten women photographers at the Heliconian Club in Toronto. Visit http://www.lindabriskinphotography.com/

Kirk Boys is a writer living outside Seattle with his wife and a tiny Mexican dog. His essays have appeared in Gravel Magazine, The Chaos Journal, Bio-Stories and will be reappearing in Bio-stories shortly. His works of fiction can be found in Storie #57/58, Per Contra and Thrice Fiction amongst others. He was a finalist in Glimmer Train New Writers contest and has a certificate in Literary Fiction from the University of Washington. He is a member of Richard Hugo House.

Josh Feit is currently a speechwriter for the Puget Sound's regional transit agency. Prior to that, Feit was the speechwriter for the Seattle mayor's office. Before working as a speechwriter, Feit was a journalist.

Art Bell was born February 19, 1955 in Lakewood, NJ, where his father was an accountant and his mother a piano teacher. He grew up learning accounting and classical piano, among other things. In high school he co-founded and edited the satirical underground newspaper, THE TONGUE. His articles in THE TONGUE got him into trouble more than once. While Art's early passion was science, he discovered the joys of economics while a student at Swarthmore College. After working as an Economist in Washington DC, Art received an MBA from Wharton Graduate School and pursued a career in television. He worked at CBS, HBO (where he founded Comedy Central), Comedy Central, and Court TV. Art's recently completed memoir is entitled, "WHAT THE HELL IS GOING ON HERE? How I Founded Comedy Central and (Almost) My Sense of Humor." It's about my eight years founding, creating, and building the Comedy Central cable channel. It will be available soon. Art currently lives in Greenwich, CT with his wife, Carrie. He enjoys playing classical and jazz piano and has recently taken up jazz drumming.

Jesse Stein is a MFA student studying Creative Writing at the School of the Art Institute of Chicago. Every Friday, he orders a cannoli, for survival, and decided to write a story that would mirror the weight of this ritual. He has been previously published in 34th Parallel Indie Lit Mag, as well as F Newsmagazine.

George L Stein is a writer and photographer living in Michigan City in Northwest Indiana. George works in both film and digital formats in the urban decay, architecture, fetish, and street photography genres. His emphasis is on composition with the juxtaposition of beauty and decay lying at the center of his aesthetic. Northwest Indiana's rust-belt legacy provides ample locations for industrial backdrops. George has been published in Midwestern Gothic, Gravel, Foliate Oak, After Hours, Hoosier Lit, Gulf Stream Magazine, 3Elements, Stoneboat, Occulum, the Gnu Journal, Iliinot Review and Darkside Magazine.

Shimon Moore is a writer, jewelry maker, and Literature professor who delights in helping others discover the power of words. You are likely to find wandering through Nature with her camera to expose the very small wonders hiding everywhere, or frazzled to the point of panic, searching for the sunglasses hiding on her head. She lives with her heroic Marine husband, two spoiled Pit Bulls, and two ninja cats that like to knock her beads into oblivion while she isn't looking.

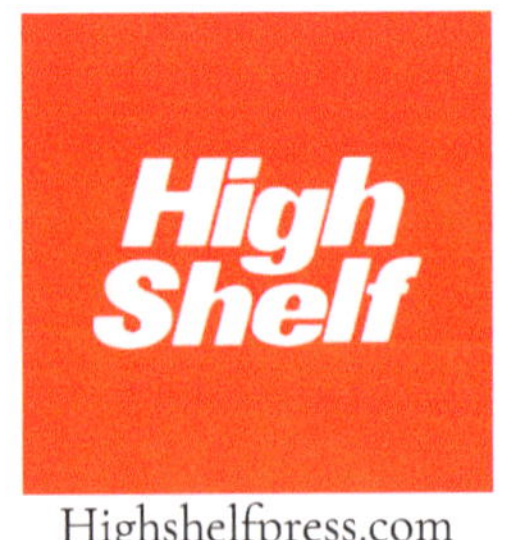

Highshelfpress.com

CPSIA information can be obtained
at www.ICGtesting.com
Printed in the USA
BVHW020808150719
553469BV00001B/12/P